CITY AS A POLITICAL IDEA

This edition first published in the United Kingdom in 2011 by University of Plymouth Press, Roland Levinsky Building, Drake Circus, Plymouth, Devon, PL4 8AA, United Kingdom.

Paperback   ISBN 978-1-84102-291-8
Hardback   ISBN 978-1-84102-292-5

© University of Plymouth Press 2011
© Krzysztof Nawratek 2011

The right of Krzysztof Nawratek to be identified as the author of this work has been asserted by him in accordance with the Copyright, Designs and Patents Act 1988.

A CIP catalogue record of this book is available from the British Library

Publisher: Paul Honeywill
Translator: Agata Pyzik
Editor: Gavin Thomas
Design: Daniel Jones, The Bridge Creative Agency

All rights reserved. No part of this publication may be reproduced, stored in a retrieval system or transmitted in any form or by any means electronic, mechanical, photocopying, recording, or otherwise, without the prior written permission of UPP. Any person who carries out any unauthorised act in relation to this publication may be liable to criminal prosecution and civil claims for damages.

Published with the Support of the Polish Cultural Institute and The Book Institute, Kraków, Poland.

Cover image © Max Pigott 2011
www.maxpigott.com

Typeset by The Bridge Creative Agency in Sabon 10/14pt
Printed and bound by Edwards Brothers, NBN International, Plymouth

CITY AS A POLITICAL IDEA

Krzysztof Nawratek

University of Plymouth Press

Foreword

Joseph Rykwert

A town, a city, is a political idea – as the title of this book asserts. Of course, it is also a physical, lived experience, and since most readers of this book will be city dwellers they will have had that experience. Many of them will have found their environment troubling and hostile, as did Krzysztof Nawratek, who wrote this book in the hope that his fellow critics will join him in changing this uncomfortable reality.

Though it is a call for change, this is no call to arms. Nawratek knows the perils of violent change. He wants pressure exercised on the financing and the governance of urban space, and a new understanding of what we can demand of it. He proposes that it be done by hacking into the systems which run 'things', into the management structure that presents itself as absolute. The acronymic slogan of this structure, 'TINA', suggests that whatever improvements we might have in mind, There Is No Alternative.

However you look at it though, alternatives do offer themselves, if only because the exponential growth of the urban fabric is not really constant. While many cities – like Shenzhen or São Paulo – do seem to expand ceaselessly, there are others that shrink. A number have done so in old East Germany, and Detroit – one of the world's great industrial centres – has lost two thirds of its population over the last sixty years while some of its fabric is riddled and perilous. Squatters occupy high-rises.

The managers who run our world, and whose belief in constant economic and industrial growth seems unshakeable, are not interested in such glitches. Yet we have to reckon with them, and with the imbalance of cities where high-rises are surrounded by spontaneous, uncontrolled and miserable suburbs.

Against that, Nawratek calls for cities which not only enable but even entice citizens to engage with each other: a city which regulates and orders neighbourly relations so that it initiates and facilitates personal interaction. And he hopes to show how such relations can be formed to foster civic virtue among its inhabitants.

This high – but attainable and wholly desirable – aim inevitably reflects on the physical fabric of the city. He offers the English reader an understanding of Belfast as well as Porto Alegre in Brazil, Manchester as well as Riga. He calls on research which the late Kevin Lynch carried out in Boston sixty years ago, when he observed how Bostonians plotted their city and how their mental map related to the way they inhabited and 'used' it. That such a readable form helps the inhabitant to feel at home in a city is too well-attested to require comment. It is, in a way, the guarantee that the social capital of trust and interdependence can flourish in it.

For the city which Nawratek proposes to construct is a city in which all participate: in which the immigrant is not an alien, and where electronic communications are no substitute for personal relations; a city where private ownership and the commercial exploitation of urban space are subsumed to the public interest and the citizen's quest for *areté*. Like him, I hope that such cities will come about, piecemeal perhaps, and without harsh sanctions. His may not be a call to arms, but it is certainly an inducement for us to change our ways.

— Joseph Rykwert

Paul Philippe Cret Professor of Architecture Emeritus at the University of Pennsylvania. Author of many important architectural works, including: *The Idea of Town* (1963) and *The Seduction of Place* (2000).

I. BEFORE
PAGE 11

II. INVISIBLE
PAGE 15

17   Citizenship
22   City as a Political Community. *Death of Polis*
29   Strangers in the City. *Immigrants as Attraction, Immigrants as Menace*
34   Social Capital
39   Fall of the Peripheral Cities. *Disposable Cities*
45   City Management. Managerial Governance against 'the Local Community'
52   'Dispersed' Power against 'Real' Power
59   Plug-in Citizen as a Prerequisite for the Resurrection of Polis.
     Polis as a Defense and Liberation

III. INTIMATE
PAGE 71

73   The Inhabitant of a Peripheral City
78   Everyday Life in a Subjective City
83   A Fugitive from a Peripheral City
88   Freedom and Alienation
93   To Live or Survive
97   The World Is Ours
101   To Each Their Own Paradise
104   A Plug-in Human Being, A-androgyne. *People Hooked by Their Shortcomings*

IV. Visible
PAGE 119

121 The Spatial Structure of Semi-peripheral Cities. *A Social-spatial Disintegration of a Postmodern City*
128 Neighbourhood Community in a Semi-peripheral City
133 The Lost Myth of the Socialist City?
138 City as Oppression
145 The Rebuilding of Polis
150 A-androgynic Space. *In Search of a Post-neoliberal City Model*
154 Happy People In Their Own City

V. After
PAGE 157

Endnotes
PAGE 161

I.
Before

Cities are growing. Not all of them and not everywhere, but the fact of their growth and increasing importance is beyond doubt. What does it actually mean, though – that cities are growing? Does it only mean that they increase their space, crawl around and devour surrounding towns and villages? Or that they increase their number of inhabitants, or grow their GDP? We know that these are the cities in which the modern world's social, economic, political and cultural lives concentrate. Cities today appear almost as powerful as ever, and yet they are in crisis. The standard of living in cities in most countries of the world is dropping dramatically, and even if – as in China – the GDP growth of some of them is close to 20%, the level and quality of city life is still not improving, and sometimes deteriorating.

People flee the cities. In the United States, so-called *urban sprawl* – the process of suburbanisation, moving to the suburbs – is in full swing. In the former GDR (German Democratic Republic), we can observe fascinating *shrinking cities*. In Poland too, more and more people want to live in the suburbs, and if possible move to a house with a garden. However, the biggest weakness in modern cities concerns the political arena. Devotees of European Cities gladly refer to the Greek *polis*, and the Polis was primarily a political concept (it is from the word *polites* – which denotes fully fledged citizens of a Polis – that the word politics comes, after all). Yet despite economic growth, despite the fact that national or international political institutions locate their headquarters in the cities, modern cities have almost no political significance in themselves. Thus, despite city planning and population growth, the Cities are dying. They die as a political idea and as a way of life for their citizens based on self-managing communities. So while at first glance it may seem that the City is experiencing staggering growth today, in fact, there is exactly the opposite process going on. Of course, the external, physical dimension of the city is growing, but what grows, what is still called the City, is not its core – it is a mutated tumor, a caricature of the City. It is an 'urbanised area' rather than the City. Cities are dying and I do not think that we can stop this process. The death of the City does not yet mean the end of the idea that the City was, that contributed to the history of Europe and the world. Cities are dying as a concept of community life but this death does not mean that the story ends. There is a life after death. The term 'urbanised area' is a description of a certain socio-spatial phenomenon, while the City was a project of political, social and economic development. Above all, political. After the death of Cities we can expect there to be something new, something that will be a new idea of themselves for people who live in large groups within small areas. The death of the City may be the resurrection of the Polis. Polis, understood as a way of managing the community which lives in the 'urban area' formerly known as the City.

The City's life after death is, above all, a political concept of how people organise their lives as a community in space. And that is what this book is about. It is not just about city urbanism, architecture, economics and hundreds of other matters which relate to cities. It is about the death of the City, its causes and signals of what it might become. This is a political book: its purpose is political.

This book would not exist but for the help and kindness of many people. I must thank my publisher, Janek Sowa, for daring to publish it in Poland; Michał Herer, for his comments and suggestions concerning the philosophical aspects of this book; Krzysztof Kafka, for our private and public discussions about urban planning, space and politics (published online at www.miejsca.org); Magdalena Piekara, for her critical comments; and Anna 'Maug' Grzybowska, for supporting me throughout the whole process of writing and thinking. Thank you also to my wife Katarzyna, without whose faith in this book, and in me, it would have not succeeded. Finally, I thank my late father, Henryk Nawratek, who first taught me to look at and think about the City.

For the new English language edition of this book, I am deeply grateful to the Polish Cultural Institute in London, the Book Institute in Kraków and the Faculty of Arts at the University of Plymouth. I would also like to thank my translator Agata Pyzik and my editor Gavin Thomas, without whose passion and patience you would not be able to share my vision today.

Thank you also to all those not mentioned here who have supported me. What is good and valuable in this book, I am happy to share with those mentioned above. For all the errors, only I am responsible.

II.

Invisible

CITIZENSHIP   II.I

What is citizenship? What is the meaning and sense of citizenship? A Citizen is a kind of a socio-political construct, whose function is to include the individual in the political system.

Citizenship is assumed, therefore, to be a neutral tool that enables man to enjoy certain rights and privileges, but also imposes certain duties on man. We must remember that the liberal idea of a Citizen (for now let us forget Greek origins) was conceived to enable man to break away from the political authority of the Church. The Citizen is abstracted from a variety of more or less natural communities (family, clan, etc.) – or, as we could see it today, from a network of dependencies – and placed in a theoretically neutral sphere of politics. In this way, the claims of all these groups are weakened because they are filtered through the abstract construct of the Citizen. This concept is one of the cornerstones of liberal thought and democracy, but we should not be subject to the illusion that this idea can be the foundation of a modern liberal-democratic society. Even if nationality itself is a neutral state – after all, the essence of citizenship is the alignment of the political rights of unequal people – the process of gaining or granting citizenship is not neutral. Citizenship can be regarded as a kind of privilege and privileges create inequalities – which is why nationality has its positive side, of inclusion in a community, but also means an exclusion from the political community of non-Citizens.[1] This exclusive power of citizenship has consequences not only in politics but also – and this is the problem that is primarily addressed in this book – in physical and social urban space.

What is citizenship? We experience it the most when we do not have it. When one is excluded from a community then one can see its strength and attractiveness. Since the entry of Poland into the European Union, Poles in many countries – those that fully opened their labour markets – no longer experience the humiliation of being illegal immigrants. They have stopped experiencing it and so they have stopped understanding it. This experience has not applied a change or extension to their citizenship – Poles are still citizens of Poland rather than Ireland, Sweden or the UK. The only change that has occurred since May 2004 is that governments, in some member countries, have created for the citizens of this new EU country career and resident opportunities *almost* on the same conditions as the citizens of those countries. And in this case, the word 'almost' really is of little importance. The right to work, the right to health and social care, along with suffrage rights in local elections comprise, practically speaking, almost the full dimension of citizenship, of which the citizens of new EU members dream.

So what is this contemporary *almost* citizenship? It is right to take roots in a community, yet the law has traditionally associated with the biological side of human existence. This so-called 'biological citizenship' is now increasingly seen as a further step of change in the understanding of citizenship – from the citizenship of the political, the social, to the new biological citizenship.[2] As such, it is more a mechanism of deterritorialisation and the subsequent uprooting of the community than it is of rooting. The mere passage of citizenship from the political dimension to the social has moved it from the sphere of loyalty – loyalty to the state and to the community (in the nineteenth century there was also the biological dimension: ethnic citizenship) – to the sphere of individual privileges. This shift in the conception of citizenship from its political significance to its social importance was, primarily, associated with Europe's burgeoning welfare state model in the years following the Second World War. However, having a green card fulfilled this dream for many immigrants in the USA. Full citizenship gave an additional freedom of movement and of smooth entry into the territories of countries that have signed agreements with the USA Visa Waiver. Citizenship – holding the passport of a country, but especially a rich country – has a tangible financial meaning, as proven by Valpy FitzGerald and J.A. Cuesta-Leiva.[3] Having a passport in some countries, however, demands certain responsibilities from the 'full' citizens – most commonly associated with knowing a language and the obligation of military service. More attractive to many immigrants seems the status of an *almost* citizen, which gives key rights and privileges without imposing the duties of 'full' citizenship.

The focus of modern citizenship, though, is on the individual rights and privileges of the citizen rather than on their duties – this shift is significant and crucial. Despite recent and quite aggressive criticism (primarily alleging 'anglocentrism' and ignoring the tensions and conflicts in multiethnic societies), a liberal understanding of citizenship conceived by Thomas Humphrey Marshall is still valid – at least from the point of view of a single person trying to be a citizen.[4] For Marshall, citizenship is in fact full participation, full connectivity with the community. This communication takes place in three areas – civil rights, political rights and social rights. The concept of citizenship formulated by Marshall is of a sociological rather than political nature. It assumes that rather than obtaining these rights passively, becoming a citizen requires a more active participation in the construction of citizenship.

Citizenship as a concept was initially designed to pull people out of their communities – religious, clan or ethnic – and place them in a neutral space of politics. Citizenship was thus primarily a destructive force, but this destruction was a very important act – such a 'stripped down' person, free from restraining bonds, was necessary for the State. So instead of 'natural' loyalty, citizenship was premised upon a 'searching' loyalty to the State – a more or less abstract being. Today, however, in a situation where many of the national States have withdrawn to neoliberal positions, loyalty to them is replaced by either ethnic and religious loyalties, or by loyalty to supranational and deteritorrialised structures – to the international organisations and large corporations.

So rightly, researchers such as Mark Purcell see opportunities for the city in this process – in changing the scale at which we perceive citizenship.[5] People could move away from the abstract to smaller and more specific communities, which is definitely a path worth considering, but we must be aware that in exchanging abstractions for concrete reality we return to a premodern situation, back to 'natural' communities and social bonds. That is what our modern liberal democratic civilisation is afraid of, and in which (quite rightly!) it sees the danger of a fresh outbreak of the war of all against all and the disintegration of our global world. Today, as discussed by Jane Jenson and Martin Papillon, citizenship is still attractive as an idea of inclusive political community, but probably in order for individuals to claim their rights or special privileges and not so that they can feel part of a larger group, unified by common values and dreams.[6] Citizenship has a similar importance in contemporary feminist discourse – it is all about equal opportunities, about hearing other voices in public debate, about extending democracy to a 'feminocratic' dimension.

So if we want to discuss the problem of citizenship in reference to the modern city, we are trapped by these contradictory meanings and interpretations. A citizen will thus wrench identity from the 'traditional' (family, clan, ethnic) networks and relationships while seeking new hooks, new areas of loyalty. Citizenship seen 'from below' will insist on inclusion in the system, the recognition of rights and granting of privileges, but nationality seen 'from above' – from the perspective of the authority of the City – will be an attempt to foster and manage an urban community that will minimise conflicts.[7] Citizenship of one or the other perspective has purely instrumental importance. However, citizenship in itself means nothing and has no inherent value. Here we touch on the problem of citizenship in urban space; today's dispute over the City is a dispute over who gets the City. Right to the City is a fundamental issue which also affects citizenship but as I mentioned above, and as argued by Christian Joppke, the concept of 'citizenship' is relevant only instrumentally.[8] The liberal understanding of citizenship proposed by Thomas Humphrey Marshall is challenged the most in multiethnic and multicultural societies, not only those in which the immigrants arrived – although in their case the weakness of citizenship is the most obvious – but also wherever 'precitizenship' social bonds are still strong. The question that arises here is – are all citizens equal, and should they be treated in the same way? A classic liberal answer would be 'yes', but this rhetoric of equality is used by both representatives of communities who feel discriminated against and by municipal authorities who use it to justify their non-alignment with movements for equality for disadvantaged communities – and it does not matter whether the discrimination is real or whether it is, like citizenship, a tool to obtain more rights and privileges.

Another issue raised by both alterglobalist movements and academia is the collapse of the so-called Westphalian order in world politics; the crisis of the liberal-democratic vision of society and the triumph of neoliberalism, reflected primarily in the overwhelming advantage that global corporations have gained over ordinary people. This neoliberal movement of power is very closely linked to the shift of content within the concept of citizenship; from the Citizen, defined by participation in a political community, in the direction of the Citizen-Consumer defined by participation in a system of neoliberal economy.[9] Catherine Needham points out several features that distinguish the Citizen-Consumer from the Citizen in the classical sense, and two of them seem crucial to me: an individualised, self-centred relationship with the System (at this stage I would prefer not to define this 'System'), and the donor-recipient roles – the relationship of a client, not a partner, and of 'interested' loyalty. The replacement of the Citizen with the Citizen-Consumer seems another 'trick' of the neoliberal system which, by severing all relationships other than those between the recipients of goods and the donors of goods, diminishes us as human beings, as Persons. If in classical philosophy, especially in the Christian philosophies, the richness and multidimensionality of human beings is being constantly emphasised, a model of the Citizen-Consumer reduces a person to their mouth, gastrointestinal tract and rectum (or other similar sequences), supplemented only by a credit card.

However, as we have seen by tracing the genesis of the idea of citizenship, such an end was written into it. I am suspicious of the Citizen as an abstract construct, detached from the Person (and therefore the human-in-context), because this by definition rejects and reduces the richness of the relationships in which we exist (or once existed?). The Citizen-Consumer, this neoliberal monster, is then an obvious consequence of the liberal Citizen. Economics devoured politics because politics turned out to be pure abstraction and illusion. From this point comes my criticism of the Citizen and an introduction to my idea of the Plug-in Citizen.

City as a Political Community
Death of Polis

Pierre Manent writes, "[City] is the idea of a public space in which people live together, consider and decide together about everything that relates to their common interests. This was, therefore, the idea of possession by a human community of the conditions of their own existence. This was quite naturally, therefore, also a political idea" – and further – "Cities [...] are 'ideologically weak'; they are something 'individual' between these two universalisms: the idea of empire and the idea of the mission of the Church."[10] The fact that the City is (also) a political being seems clear, but mostly this politicisation is now understood as the presence of structures and institutions external to the City – of the national state or international organisations. Alternatively, the city is understood as a structure within which to place the political process. The City is then more a decoration than a participant in these processes. It is interesting that the classic understanding of the City as Polis formulated by Aristotle – that is, a primarily political being, a concept in which a certain group of people together have authority over a certain space – now seems to be highly problematic. This is probably because, as correctly formulated by Lefebvre, it is extremely difficult to identify the community in the modern city.[11] His dramatic question – to whom does the city belong? – means that yes, we follow the political process in the city, but the City itself is rather a space for policy, not a political idea in itself.[12] Even worse, Agamben points at the camp rather than the City as the fundamental biopolitical paradigm of the Western world.[13] Is the loss of the City, as a potential model of political community, thus a basic drama which results in a loss of community as a whole? Or at least a sense of loss in the belief that the community can produce root units without losing its universal dimension? That the community is the choice of the person rather than a weight of oppression over the individual? But what happens with cities today? What is their position, and why are cities no longer Polis today?

States are falling apart: functionally, where some fragments are beginning to be more strongly associated with global institutions than the state; or spatially, where cross-border cooperation gives rise to functional regions more strongly associated with each other than with the countries in which they are located. For example, let us consider Tallinn, whose development is to a significant degree driven by Helsinki and Bratislava. It is trying to maintain some independence from Vienna, stressing competition more than cooperation, but it does not matter which strategy the weaker city adopts – cooperation or controlled competition – the effect is similar. What follows is a slow stretching of the structures of these cities and the retraction of the weaker states in the structure of the stronger countries. Unofficial Helsinki government pressure on the authorities of Tallinn is a widely known and commented upon reality. But the cities – in themselves – also disintegrate, either due to internal social and economic inequalities (guarded settlements or simply better and worse neighbourhoods), or because of external factors (sometimes regional, sometimes global) which bind parts of cities into a network, leaving other parts to waste. Global cities in the so-called developing countries – to name just São Paulo, Johannesburg and Calcutta – have shown that unbelievable poverty and social tragedy can exist alongside richness and full participation in the global world.

The key moment in which the city began to decay spatially – because social diversity has always existed – came with the emergence of *nonlinear* transport, and especially the loss of importance afforded to pedestrian traffic. Currently, we are moving from place to place ever more efficiently, but the space between the area in which we are and the area in which we want to be is becoming increasingly less important. The only things of importance are the entry points and exit points. Another key factor is the global information network – made of telecommunications systems such as TV, mobile phones and the Internet. It connects us to people, ignoring their locations and, more importantly, creating a more and more virtual, extrageographical realm. Traditional mass media like TV and radio, broadcast from central facilities, are still the most important source of information – they are unrivalled in terms of rumor and direct interpersonal communication. But on the other hand, the power of 'alternative' information, transmitted by emails or Twitter, is worth analysis. Different kinds of 'analogue virus' – a drawing, a plea for help, a joke – are sent between friends at an amazing rate all over the world. For now, these things are mostly copied without possessing any special quality or quantity of content, but I would venture to say that this way of transmitting information through a 'virtual rumor' may become an important component of an 'alternative' world of information. More likely, however – although pessimistic – seems the opinion that it will just be another tool of manipulation.

More and more people are becoming parts of the network – tied to different organisations that are no longer a whole. Of course, people have always functioned as parts of different subsystems, but never have these subsystems been so separated from each other. This involvement in various organisations in different subsystems makes a person cease to be an integral person, and instead become a 'functionate' – Catholic, Buddhist, member of a corporation, union or association of Barbie collectors. This loss of integrity disturbs both the institutional religions, which recognise the cracks in their believers who are living 'parallel lives' – the religious and laic people – and also the corporations that are striving to organise the lives of their employees, leaving them no room for private passions. All those meetings organised by the company – for training or play – are an attempt to subjugate the whole person, and not just a portion thereof functioning as an employee. However, if the religions – no matter what our attitude to their views – try to see a person in their many dimensions (albeit with an eschatological perspective), the corporations have the perspective of economic efficiency, and a person is only a narrowly specialised (although very complicated) tool for this efficiency.

So today, people either fall to pieces or become a 'narrow specialised' – members of sects, corporate employees, etc. Organisations, institutions and groups have an increasingly extrageographical character. Globalisation – the 'netting' of people who have a close relationship – is a dubious boon. Without prejudging whether more people benefit from globalisation or lose out, the fact is that many of the poor people of this world are in exploitation networks rather than exchange networks. As Michael Edwards notes, however, it is also true that some kind of 'global civil society' seems to be emerging.[14] However, it seems that most of these organisations concern the Western world, the rich world who can afford – financially and mentally – to begin to consider problems that are global and not just national. Edwards also writes about the organisations associated with the 'poor world', mostly about Shack/Slum Dwellers International (SDI), but despite global coverage these organisations are focused primarily on local activity, on specific communities in a particular area.

But the disintegration of urban space of which I write, is it – in itself – bad? In Riga, a legend is told. From time to time, from the Daugava river which flows through the City, a Monster emerges who asks: "Has the City been completed yet?" The answer, which should be immediately given to him, is: "No!" – because a prophecy says that when the City is completed then it shall be destroyed. This legend is an excellent illustration of a very important feature of City – every City is a process. It does not become a completed project. Therein lies the basic difference between architecture and urbanism – architecture relates to finite structures (buildings), whereas urbanism concerns entities that appear and disappear. If buildings (and therefore architecture) are fighting against time, against the passing of time, then they are contrary to City: City has time as its ally. The City is change. The City is thus a Deleuzian diagram, recorded in matter and space, but time is not the only important element when thinking about this place. In the legend, as I mentioned, a 'lack' is important: an 'imperfection' or 'incompleteness' that is not evil but – quite the contrary – gives it life, a guarantee of being as such, while 'perfection' is synonymous with destruction. Referring to the Christian concept of love, Slavoj Žižek wrote that "incompleteness, in a sense, stands higher than the completeness."[15] City confirms this view because 'incompleteness' and 'imperfection' does not mean decay. The City is diversity. After all, Aristotle argued that the City consists of people of various kinds. Alike people cannot create a city. For Aristotle, City is a partnership which involves the interaction of people living in the city. Furthermore, according to Aristotle, City is founded on the interests of virtue and its task is the 'education' of its citizens. The City, therefore, also in the classical sense, is a dynamic entity. The City is to educate, and so the City is something that works – not just something that lasts.

The City as such – and this will be another attempt to define the City – is a permanent revolution. In this way, we return once again to politics. The City is pure potential, but always loses and regains its potentiality. The City continues to be expanded and rebuilt. It is still being destroyed and is still being created. Can the City then be a model, an example, a starting point for more fundamental considerations? Before we attempt this path, let us consider potentiality a while longer. Emptiness calls for a fulfillment. Lack calls for a restoration. But fulfillments or supplements never leave us completely satisfied. Almost always, we feel that by filling the canvas, the notebook pages, land in the city or, in the end, our lives with a kind of content, we kill all the other – perhaps better – opportunities. Creativity, or simply 'being', kills potentiality. Life is a desperate loss of opportunities. Instead of experiencing the infinite potentials of existence, most of us fill our lives with one in particular. Are we sure that it is the best possibility? Uncertainty about the value of our existence is an indelible feature of our lives. What does this have to do with the City? The City is – to some extent – forever. We have (though perhaps not everyone will agree with this view) one life. The City experiences itself in many ways. Certain spatial arrangements – the roads, squares, and quarters marked out in Roman times – persist and continue to organise the City today, despite the fact that everything else – people, social systems, economic and political climates – has changed. But of course, in a given place and time, there is only that one single City.

That is how the City exists in itself, but it is only from one perspective – the second, equally important aspect concerns how the City exists for its residents. The area of the City which each of us uses is very small. No matter whether we live in a big city or small town, the space in which we exist is quite clearly defined. Of course, some of us are more active than others, but all of us are subject to certain restrictions – we cannot be in several places at the same time; moving around the city will take some time; our lives are often structured around a triangle of work or school, family, and fun, friends or shopping. Of course, we sometimes want to break the monotony of our journey and go to a district in which we have never been, but – let's be honest – this is extremely rare. So if a City, and what we need to consume from it, can be so small – then are large cities in general unnecessary?

The fact that our needs in the City are limited is the primary cause of both its decay and the success of the disurbanising processes, and especially so-called *urban sprawl* and the emergence of suburbs stretching to tens of kilometers. Most of us dream of a house with a garden, most of us have to work (or in our youth, learn) and if we go shopping it is best combined with going to the cinema, bowling and drinking coffee with a friend. In this way, an operating scheme of a typical inhabitant of the American city is created (but also of the City of which most Europeans dream – please visit Dublin, Riga and the cities of East Germany). The fact is that European cities have a different structure, due primarily to historical reasons as well as economic conditions – not everyone can afford a house and not everyone wants to commute for hours. But let us return briefly to those tiny 'subjective towns' in which each of us live. What do they have in common? Common shops? Industries? Cinemas? This is a crucial moment – we are talking here not so much about urban space as we are about urban communities. About the Community which has disappeared. Indeed, what unites people living in one city? People who, in the classic Aristotelian sense, should create Polis? Is there any urban community in general? Or is there only political community?

A central public space – the archetypal agora, a place of honor – was the essence of a traditional City, but even if public spaces still exist in our cities, and even when creating new plazas, arcades and urban parks, their meaning is closely linked to commercialism or the health and welfare of residents. Public spaces in our cities today have no political, but merely commercial-entertainment significance. There was indeed – as I wrote in the previous chapter – an important international shift in political and economic climates, and Catherine Needham rightly speaks of the 'Citizen-Consumer' (with a decisive emphasis on 'Consumer'). That is the key problem of modern cities – the disappearance of the political community. The collapse of public spaces and their replacement with commercial spaces, the disintegration of the urban structure and privatisation of its spaces are results, not causes. There was a complete dehiscence of the City space along with the political idea of the City.

Why is the disappearance of the political community crucial in understanding the crisis of the City? Because the lack of a political community is the lack of *any* community. As Jadwiga Staniszkis writes, "too big a withdrawal of the state may not only lead to 'denationalisation', but also 'desocialisation' (because people are beginning to see their 'citizenship' as irrelevant to their own fate)."[16] What connects the City's inhabitants? Shopping together in a suburban mall? The fact that we were all in a multiplex once? So what? The potential in this cinema or that shop to meet others? That's clearly absurd.

Rebuilding the local community, the community at district level, seemed to offer some hope for the disappearance of the political community from the City as a whole – however, even at this level the community disappears. Nothing unites people living side-by-side. Therefore, the *subjective cities* are first a political and social problem, only then a spatial one. The reintegration of urban space cannot be carried out with urban tools. Urbanism, as such, or land use planning are increasingly irrelevant, precisely because their role has become purely regulatory, instrumental and expert. One cannot save the cities through interventions and social programs either – it is still too little; these are only half measures. The only effective remedy would be to reclaim the City as a political idea, as a self-governing organism. Not planning, not social programs, but *politics* is the path of salvation for cities.

STRANGERS IN THE CITY II.III
Immigrants as Attraction, Immigrants as Menace

The issues concerning immigration and multiethnicity are extremely broad. In addition to these is the problem of 'other Others' in the City. The different groups in the City, though they have a great joint role, also have a lot of overlap. 'Strangers' in the city are not necessarily immigrants – for instance, strangers in the city of a conservative society can be homosexuals, who after all come from within that same society, while immigrants under certain conditions (for example, in the cities where immigrants make up the majority) are not necessarily 'strangers'. For an even better rendering of the complexity of this problem, there should be a distinction between the several types of immigrant presence in the world. Probably the simplest classification is a division into those who, with their own will or against it, stay in a 'foreign' city permanently, and those who are in such a city 'temporarily', where that period of time, though it may last for several years, is in fact – at least in the declarations of immigrants – a minor interruption in their 'proper' life. This 'temporary' migration has one primary goal – economic. Its purpose is to allow the immigrant to earn enough money to start a 'real' life upon returning to their country.

These kinds of immigrants are very strongly associated with the country of their origin and very weakly with the country in which they are temporarily staying. Most do not know (or know very little of) the language of their host country, do not want or do not have too much capacity to integrate with a culturally alien environment, and perform the simplest and worst paid work (although, of course, we have here a unique group of highly specialised workers who are often a cosmopolitan community, familiar with the language of their host country and who feel just as 'at home' or just as 'foreign' as anywhere else in the world). Their importance to the host country is basically economic; because these people are doing work which the 'locals' do not wish to pursue, there is a kind of symbiosis. To their apparent mutual satisfaction, the immigrants work and the 'locals' use them. Poles were such immigrants for many years (and still some of my countrymen remain so), as were Turks in Germany, Hispanics in the U.S. or Vietnamese in Poland.

This category of immigrants rather smoothly intertwines with another: the category of immigrants who were forced to leave their homes without being in any way prepared. I am talking about all kinds of political and economic refugees who, like those of the first category, are usually poorly educated, do the worst work, but do not have the possibility of returning to their home country. These two categories of people are, either actually or mentally, very strongly connected with their home countries and very poorly with their current country of residence. It is obvious that the image of the country held by its guest is different on the 'outside' – when dealing with family and friends – than on the 'inside'. For family and friends that remained in the homeland, the country in which an immigrant is staying is almost a paradise, whereas the reality of the 'inside' is the complete opposite – it is mostly hell. On the other hand there are immigrants who confidently choose their 'second homeland' and often find relationships (marriage, partnerships or friendships) with the 'locals', who then in turn smoothly merge with a group of refugees who for various reasons do not want to have anything to do with their country of origin at all.

Since all these categories of immigrants and 'foreigners' are mixed together, I would like to distinguish my area of interest in this chapter very clearly. A key problem here is – as throughout the whole book – the roots: the relationship between the human being, the society and space. Therefore, I will treat all other distinctions as secondary, focusing primarily on the relationship between the person with their place of residence and the place (or places) that is 'external'. With this perspective, City residents appear to us as beings with no race, no gender or other such parameters, situated instead on the excluded—included axis. But before we can answer the question: "Why are some city residents more excluded than others?" – and we can be sure that we would have to give a specific answer in any case – we must notice that such an action takes place at all. At this point, however, some doubt must appear – if I have mentioned immigrants who are in fact 'rooted' in their places of origin, must this exclusion be in any case destructive and tragic? Maybe instead of thinking about the exclusion of one particular space we should actually generalise it even more in this case? And simply ask about the exclusion proliferating in the world? But let us leave that question for now – though it is fundamental to this book.

Meanwhile, back to those excluded from the (physical and social) City space. The fact is that those born in the town are usually in a better position, are more 'rooted' in this space. They know the area; they are familiar with the paths, roads, squares and shops. They know the people. They have the enemy-friend system adjusted accordingly. However, the family into which they were born and the area in which they grew up is even more important. Perhaps a native to London's Kensington area will not feel too confident in the East End and Southwark, but because they come from a particular part of the city, have certain parents and friends, they will be firmly and permanently rooted in the city (as a whole, or in its 'better' and 'major' part). Today, it is social position, wealth, influence and power that are the true causes of being rooted in the world. Roots in the City are no longer afforded as much significance in the eyes of the local community. They are lost because the City is not a community anymore. The idea that the City is a political community was European – in China, a city resident was still primarily a member of the clan. Their roots in the world were not geographical but social. Perhaps for this reason, Chinese ethnic neighbourhoods are still incredibly strong and unique. The legend of the 'Chinese districts' as dangerous places – a bit mysterious, but fascinating and important for the American cities, especially for their 'mythology' – can become the point at which we move from an analysis of how the Root is viewed from the inside in consideration of their lack of rootedness, and how they are seen from the outside, to a reflection on being uprooted as a tourist. However brutal it may sound, otherness is fascinating. Provided, of course, that this 'otherness' is under some control.

Districts – Chinese, Italian, Jewish and red light districts – are the spaces inhabited by people whose roots in the City are weaker than most of the inhabitants of other, perhaps better districts. In most of these places such ethnically specific people find their roots outside the City, in their families and religion. Their presence, however, is necessary for the City. The strength of the City lies in its diversity: in potential tensions between people, groups and neighbourhoods. The City is an Exchange Machine, and the separate 'districts of the uprooted' (in the City) have a threefold purpose. First, to provide for the City employees who are able to accept the unacceptable conditions necessary for an embedded population. This is because the uprooted districts operate with a certain autonomy in relation to the rest of the urban organism. The rules that prevail in them are not exactly the rules of the City, and are connected primarily with lower housing prices and generally lower maintenance prices.

In the history of Polish cities, there is the phenomenon of autonomous areas; areas separated from the city administration – 'spheres of free trade', as we would say today. The idea behind jurisdictions, special economic spheres and uprooted districts is economically the same; it is a kind of parasitic or symbiotic relationship with the City that functions independently, a separate socio-spatial structure within the city. Secondly, districts of the uprooted, due to their links with communities outside the City, become a specific transfer channel of information, people and goods to the City, from the world and back (sometimes on the border of legality, occasionally beyond it). Third, districts of the uprooted become a tourist attraction, which in modern cities is extremely important. This even applies to notorious neighbourhoods such as New York's Harlem.[17] Minorities who live in ethnic neighbourhoods may be anywhere between the City elites and the margins of society. The so-called 'middleman minority' economic niches are filled, ensuring a fairly rapid generation and retention of revenue in the social and economic structure of cities.[18] For example, Korean communities who addressed this issue in 1992, to the great rancour of the African-American population during the famous riots in Los Angeles, illustrate this process perfectly and display immigrants who threaten the city.

Denis Judd writes: "In the poststructuralist literature dealing with the city, enclaves (districts) are understood as local hubs of international capital and cultural structures, hiding behind a mask of locality: gated communities, through the magic of marketing, are becoming the neighbouring units, shopping malls are the new marketplaces, and neighbourhoods offer a simulacrum of authentic tourist cities, which they are replacing."[19] If on such a structure of cities – with strong vertical links to the outside world – we superimpose these districts of the uprooted, particularly ethnic neighbourhoods, we get a picture of the City which is – de facto – only a local representation of the forces and structures existing outside it. The City has lost almost entirely its local nature and situates its meaning almost entirely outside itself. The residents are rooted against 'their' city in a transcendent way. The European model of City as an autonomous entity is replaced by a kind of quasi-colonial city. Analogies with colonial cities are of course only partial, but such an image is firmly in favour with the imagination.

The city becomes the space colonised by various entities, groups and forces external to its residents, whose interests and roots lie out of town. Suddenly it is occupied by both big corporations and illegal immigrants. The only 'true' residents of the city to remain are the poor, pushed to the margins and forced to feed off the dumping ground of globalisation. However, even these groups are trying to escape the city. Inside the city, the local poor are trying to become global paupers (the flight from the cities that I have already discussed).

Then what is the role of immigrants in the City? Everything depends on their area of rooting. Immigrants who are able to fit the slots of the City, and fill the existing social and economic niches without losing the ties to their place of origin, can achieve relative success and stability. Frequently, they occupy better positions in the City than some of its native inhabitants. If, however, for various reasons the bond with their home country is poor, and the city in which they live has a socially and economically compact, tight structure, the immigrants fall to the bare bottom of the social hierarchy. They become modern slaves, exploited without mercy. They also become 'invisible' to the rest of the urban society, and so the city does not make use of the valuable culture they bring, but uses only their bodies as an extremely cheap and efficient workforce. Sooner or later this huge injustice results in outbursts of hatred (as in France during 2005), but primarily it works as a demoralising force on the city itself.

Social Capital

Social capital is a concept of rather fluid definition. Generally, however, we can say that social capital is a network of (positive) social ties based on mutual trust, which enable the functioning of both civil society and capitalist economy. Contrary to what might occur to 'capitalists' (and 'politicians'), the functioning of a free economy is very difficult without mutual trust. Edward Glaeser believes that intellectual flows – the ideas circulating among individuals that are not subject to the mediation of the market – are the foundation of economic growth.[20] Similarly, 'public trust' is a very general definition of social capital, as social capital flourishes best where there is not much physical capital. This happens mainly in poor countries (to mention microcredits and the 2006 Nobel Peace Prize laureate Muhammad Yunus, founder of Grameen Bank, who pioneered institutional money lending to the extremely poor), and also occurred in the People's Poland. Social capital is usually territorial. Strong relationships between people mainly concern those living side-by-side. There is something of the original instinct here, which concentrates animals in a dense crowd in times of danger. This is because social capital is 'primitive'. It applies mostly to ordinary people seeking help and is rooted in the natural communities of family or clan, usually very religious.

In short – social capital is strong, whereas the single person is weak. Social capital was, for example, quite well circulated in People's Poland around the tower block estates – people borrowed flour and sugar from each other, and watched each other's children. But these relationships and the trust implicit in them disappeared when the 'real' capital emerged. It is clear that – as Aihwa Ong writes in her latest book – capitalism (or better, neoliberalism) devours everything.[21] Social capital, as a relic of the industrial society (and earlier) is also criticised by Richard Florida.[22] The mere notion of inventing a creative capital and designating spaces for 'outsiders' (people who do not fit the standards of the conservative society) suggests that social capital is an outdated idea, and with all its 'hard' social ties a dangerous and harmful one at that. In fact, social capital actually has its dark side: gangs, the mafia, nepotism and 'cronyism'. Social capital is often tied to the institutionalised religions and, while on the one hand religious communities can often lend a hand to those in need, they are also linked with intolerance, fanaticism and sometimes – at least symbolic – violence. It is no coincidence that Hamas in Palestine owes its popularity not so much to the armed struggle as to its charitable activities.[23] A similar mechanism has led to the authority of the Turkish Justice and Development Party, or the two major parties in Northern Ireland: DUP (Democratic Unionist Party) and Sinn Féin. It is no wonder that Florida, who claims that the basis of 'creative capital' is tolerance (as well as talent and technology), sees social capital as a threat to urban development in the twenty-first century and more of a problem than an opportunity. So described, social capital would thus be associated with a territorially defined self-help and self-control society.

Maybe we would all be happy in a world where self-help and selfless benevolence prevailed over the religiously or ideologically motivated desire to control what our peers do, say and think, but social self-control is an inherent feature of social capital. It is hard to entirely reject or condemn this social self-control. Cases which have been reported in the press where children, people with disabilities, women or the elderly are abused for years by their families – with a total lack of interest by their neighbours, police, social services or anyone – show that social self-control is not just a case of looking for neighbours under the covers or inside closets, and that its absence can cost lives. Perhaps because of all these concerns and perspectives, social capital is a concept so difficult to define and unilaterally reject as a relic of the past that the relic as proposed by Florida – which is incompatible with liberal-democratic postindustrial (capitalist) social formations – seems to me an abuse. Tolerance, which is the foundation of a liberal-democratic consensus – and which Florida sees as a basic unification of 'soft' social bonds, and the soil from which creative capital may emerge (this point is very important because it demystifies Florida as a radical supporter of capitalism) – also has a disadvantage: tolerance often degenerates into indifference. Nobody will give you a hand in need. Nobody will react when you are abused. Nobody will help you for free. The advantage of tolerance is precisely its weakness; tolerance is emotionally cold. Tolerance does not result in pogroms but it rarely prevents them. The reluctance of liberals to embrace social capital is easy to understand. It does not necessarily translate directly into economic growth and sometimes blocks it, because each 'good deed' done selflessly is an anarchist attack on the GDP. Social capital affects the quality of life, but not necessarily economic growth. Social capital was used to fill the gaps left by the failings of capitalism during its industrial phase but today, when everything – even emotions and affection – must be bought or sold, it has become an obstacle to the development of capitalism. Here, postmodern and postindustrial Florida is different from Glaeser.

I am interested in social capital primarily in the context of space – so let us return to the City. Areas in which social capital is in bloom are the neighbourhoods most forgotten by God, people, and (thank goodness) planners and city officials. The neoliberal city does not have the available space for them and recent events in Copenhagen, relating to the sale and then destruction by the buyer of the historic house of culture in the district of Christiania, are proof of this. It is worth considering the aforementioned transition of the citizen into the consumer. The dominance of one-dimensional perceptions of the world – that only recognise the maxims of economic efficiency and GDP growth – makes any discussion about the City as a political community lose its meaning. Because if it is not your quality of life but the amount of money in your bank account that is the only measure of your being, any such discussion must lead to the admiration of the free market and neoliberalism. If the neoliberal model is not working as its followers would like it to, it is because these assumptions are not subject to discussion – it has no alternative. It can and must improve, but there is no rejection of its underlying problems. Neoliberalism needs the city as a space and an administration, but not as a community. It is not just the domination of economy over everything else: it is a new kind of rationalism that superimposes the market rules onto 'everything else'.[24] Terror of GDP and economic efficiency pervades all aspects of a city's existence. Willingly or not, I come to the critique of capitalism. For now I shall leave it as an unspoken assumption, without specifying either the extent or the nature of this criticism.

Designing urban space, we can easily imagine the 'neoliberal' spaces – ones in which 'public' space is replaced by a 'space of consumption' (just count the number of free benches around parks and town squares, and then the places in the cafe gardens). We can also imagine a 'social space' – 'social' housing complexes like Park Hill council estate, built in Sheffield in the early 1960s and also Europe's largest listed building, were inspired by the examples of Sweden, Finland and Germany. Perhaps we could also imagine a 'creative space' – though there are not many examples of such space. But can we actually imagine a democratic space? A space which each resident could potentially plug themselves into? The question is intimate – are we ourselves able to accept everyone? Social capital is linked to a specific spatial structure of cities. I mentioned in the previous chapter that ethnic neighbourhoods are the most spatially thick and dense in terms of interpersonal interaction. In his essay *The Vital Businesses of Immigrants*, Peter Elmlund wrote: "Racism is not the problem. On the contrary, the ability of immigrants to generate a varied economy of small businesses has the potential to revitalise declining cities. But the Swedish model, like others in Europe, is still dominated by large scale modernist planning, which creates forlorn suburbs, segregates people and strangles economic growth."[25] This explains (in terms of a single factor, of course) the relative success of immigrant integration in Britain, which succeeded (although not completely) in avoiding the errors of Modernist continental urbanism, and the surprising dramas of Parisian suburbs which culminated in an explosion of social hatred in 2005.

The 'premodern' spatial structure of cities in the UK (but also Chinese neighbourhoods in the United States), which allows them to cope much better with the 'postmodern' challenges of mass immigration, is in an interesting way connected to Jadwiga Staniszkis' thesis about the greater efficiency of premodern methods of governance in the U.S. and China, in comparison with the 'modern' and 'rational' in Europe. Peter Elmlund is a traditionalist, yearning for historical, premodern structures, but reaching similar conclusions about the necessity of 'dense' spaces as the architects and city planners – whom one cannot in any way accuse of being traditionalists – such as the guru Rem Koolhaas. In his book *Content* he presents a draft for the CBD (Central Business District) in Beijing, where instead of the typical high-rise buildings he offers two types of structure – one recalling the classical quarters and the second being a megastructure. Both have something that the traditional office districts did not have: interaction densities.

So what is the significance of social capital in modern cities, and what might it be in Polis? Again, I quote Staniszkis: "It turned out that for the state to act, it needs a 'social infrastructure of power'. Without this, it is powerless. This society, functioning as a community (local, as in the U.S., or more abstract, united by a common code of communication, such as in the Netherlands), and not guns, determine the strength of the state." Social capital was necessary in the era of industrial capitalism, is still necessary today in order to fill the gaps left in countries that operate in the global capitalist system (it is thus understandable that the Nobel Prize awarded for Yunus' microcredits was a peace award), and will also be needed in the resurrected Polis. Acknowledging as partially right the critics of social capital, I will defend it for two reasons: first, social capital is in fact the only capital that can exist outside the capitalist system. Social capital, as I said, does not convert directly into cash. The second reason is emotion, which is associated with social capital. If 'the state exists primarily in the imagination', then let us add: 'and only when stimulated by emotion'. Without emotion there is nothing. There is no person or society.

FALL OF THE PERIPHERAL CITIES
Disposable Cities

Today's world is a world of cities. Cities continue to grow and it seems that nothing is able to stop this process, but besides growing cities there are many that are shrinking.[26] There are also cities that are held in suspension – failing to make the step towards metropolitan and global cities, but with the capacity to sustain themselves without shrinking – and do not collapse. Not only will the shrinking cities collapse; all the world's cities are decaying from within – contrary to appearances, growth and health – along with the fall of City. They are becoming the local representatives of global forces and structures, but this process is most noticeable in semi-urban and peripheral areas. Semi-peripheral cities are those with ambitions to become globally recognised (because the term 'global city', in the sense that is given by the Globalisation and World Cities Study Group and Network of the University of Loughborough, GaWC, is not fully adequate) but which lack the capabilities to do so. They are associated with a lack of sufficient human resources, economic and geographical peripherality, and a lack of tourist attractions that could otherwise – by increasing the 'fluctuating' population – fill gaps in their human and economic potential. There is, however, a way to build global position – and we can turn to Hong Kong for an example – that involves the use of human resources associated with the city but not its residents. Indeed, tourism is increasingly acknowledged as a major output which the poor semi-peripheral city can no longer afford to ignore. The case of Bilbao (with its most famous, though not only attraction: the Guggenheim Museum by Frank Gehry) is the best and most inspiring – because successful – example here. The case of Bilbao also illustrates what I understand by the term 'globally recognisable city' because Bilbao does not fulfil the criteria for classification as a global city by the GaWC, despite being a well known and popular city. Tourism as a tool for growth, however, also has its dark side – in fact, it creates a huge amount of very low paid and unskilled jobs. On this basis, it is difficult to build the global position of a city.

Cities grow and become increasingly important actors on the stage of the world economy. 'Urban citizenship' projects are being spoken about more and more, which seems to indicate the growing political ambitions of large cities who are trying to discount their economic success, and economic and cultural importance. Exactly – large. For it is only the big cities, global cities, that grow and get richer. Others die. Interestingly, the process of shrinking cities does not only apply to small cities. In former East Germany this process is one of the most dramatic in the world. A medium sized city – with seemingly huge growth potential – is dying.

The situation is different in Polish cities. Above all, Poland has one of Europe's highest rates of polycentric cities. The spatial structure of Polish cities is much more balanced than that of many of our neighbours – especially that of the more centralised Latvia – where the power of capital is overwhelming. Economically, and in terms of human resources, Riga comprises half of Latvia. Similar patterns can be seen in Estonia, Slovakia, Hungary and the Czech Republic. The spatial structures of Spain and Portugal are also considerably more centralised than the spatial structure of Poland. The position of Warsaw in Poland – from an economic and demographic point of view – is balanced by other centres. Each of the existing regional centres – Tricity, Wrocław, Poznań (barely, but still) and Silesia – have a chance to become important centres on a European scale. However, this has not happened because of the centralist tendencies of Warsaw and the animosity of local governments, as well as a provincial way of thinking that limits minds to the Polish territory and fails to acknowledge the existence of potential future scenarios.

But this is only a digression – most important is the fact that, in contrast to Germany, the process of shrinking is only just beginning in the Polish cities, and relates more to the outflow of population movement in the centre and periphery than to the suburbs or neighbouring municipalities. Or rather, I am concerned because the mass emigration of Poles changes the situation of Polish cities in an obvious way – population outflow is already beginning to be noticeable. Wrocław, for example, even organised a campaign to promote the city, aimed at attracting a young, skilled workforce, necessary for the investments proliferating outside Wrocław. The same process has for many years set the rhythm of life in smaller towns and cities in the Opole region, and others near the German border. Many cities in the Opole region – and increasingly in other areas of Poland – seem to exist in two phases: one lasts almost all year, when the city is asleep – and appears almost dead. The second exists in the moments when people employed in Germany, Holland, Ireland, Great Britain, Sweden, etc. come home to visit their families.

If the big cities – and the capital accumulating in them, both financial and human – are becoming stronger, then small towns are losing that capital. The strength of the city, what makes it such a great machine for growth, is its social and economic diversity. In a big city with limited space there are countless processes of growth, development and decline. However, the concentration and diversification of these processes means that they naturally interact, reinforcing or mutually stimulating each other and often – brutal though it may sound – devouring one another. This diversity and abundance only exists from a certain moment. The city only becomes real – becomes 'City' – when the number of exchange processes exceeds a certain limitation. Of course, such a definition of the city is quite arbitrary because the city (in the sense of an administrative unit) is usually defined in terms of its number of residents – indeed, it looks quite different in different countries. Population is of great (perhaps even decisive) significance, but millions of people concentrated in a small space are still a crowd, not a city. These statements reflect the point I have made several times before, that small and medium sized cities are dying because they stand out from the 'natural' organic network of dependencies. Big cities, however, are becoming part of a wider network. Their links with other cities – institutions operating on a global scale, large international companies and even countries (with which, though they have their own problems, the city continues to interact) – make them cease to have a consistent, recognisable structure. Cease to be autonomous beings. At first glance it seems completely natural, even obvious and inevitable. Is the whole world not becoming a single network? Are state networks not a network economy?

Cities become hubs of economic flows and relationships – that is their economic strength and potential for growth. The more this spider's thread is focused at a single point in space, the richer and more economically powerful the city becomes. This power and wealth, however, is to some extent illusory, and may be better defined as virtual. Since wealth lies in the networks, the economic power of the city is in fact temporary. This wealth is not rooted in the City – it simply passes through it. Manuel Castells writes about this, coming to the obvious conclusion that the city does not actually exist anymore. The traditional structure of settlement networks (described by Walter Christaller) was based on a hierarchy of trade and mutual dependence. This structure existed in a much more limited space, delineated by the possibilities of traveling from one medium to another, than the contemporary structure. It is the so-called 'ecological footprint' of the city, the area in which the city 'feeds' that was once the area most adjacent to the city. Today – especially in the large cities – we find a global footprint. It is split and fragmented. Often, the relationships between the cities themselves – even if those cities are on different continents – are stronger and more important than the cities' relationships with their peripheries. A classic example is NY-LON, the relationship between the City of London and New York's Wall Street, which is almost symbiotic. This rupture (or in any event a strong weakening) of spatial relationships between strong cities and their surroundings is a fundamental threat to small and medium sized cities. And here is a paradox: the more global a city is, the stronger it becomes, but its links with traditional – and one might say 'natural' – 'stock' weaken.

So if it is the case that the bigger cities grow, the less they need the towns and cities that have been traditionally associated with them, then the primary question becomes a matter of identifying the natural and significant relationships existing in the modern world. These links are, of course, capital ties. They do not apply, however, only to the large corporations. According to a report by UNESCO, the second largest flow of money in the world economy (the first one concerns oil) is the money sent by migrants to their countries of origin. The money that banks get from this is significant, despite there being a powerful addition to their revenues from the direct stream of capital flows that never stop anywhere.

In the short term, this movement of capital otherwise 'in exile' is one of the most important factors that could save small towns. It is worth pausing for a moment to consider a rescue technique for small towns, which will lead us to more fundamental questions. To allow the influx of capital 'in exile' to really become an opportunity for development in small towns, it has to be stimulated and involved in a broad program of 'binding' residents with these places. That is what I meant earlier when mentioning the development of Hong Kong, and its use of the loyalty of people who are not current residents. A kind of loyalty to place, to the 'brand' of the town, is essential. Nobody sends money to (and thus no one invests in) a place with which they do not feel a bond. Therefore, the binding of emigrants to their home cities must be one of the key strategies in raising the capital needed for their development. To some extent, this is already happening in certain places – the best example is the 'three for one' program run by Mexico. It is premised on the fact that three institutions (state, city and bank) add three U.S. dollars between them to each dollar that an emigrant invests in 'social infrastructure'. These cities have to offer something different; something unique, something that will make people who are leaving them want to maintain a certain connection. At this point we come to the core issues. Cities (as any company or species) grow if they manage to find an 'ecological niche'. This uniqueness is very common in the area – as Sharon Zukin calls it – of a symbolic economy. The often invoked (and often imitated, at least in plans) example of Bilbao – whose construction of that spectacular museum by Frank Gehry has changed its status from a provincial town associated with the Basque nationalist group ETA, to that of a globally recognisable city of art and culture – should be well understood. It was not the museum, or other investments in iconic architecture, that changed the status of the city. It is Gehry's uniqueness and exotic appeal – as well as that of the ETA – that is being manipulated and sold. New museums in London will not change the way that this city is perceived by the world. Even the most spectacular architectural investments in Sheffield, Plymouth and Cardiff will not become drivers of change unless they are part of a strategy of uniqueness.

Let us return to the issue of immigrants. For each individual, the place where they have lived for a long time becomes unique. It becomes a place of remembrance, stories and fantasies. These migrants are not only an obvious source of capital, but also the best advocates of their cities in the world and – perhaps above all – potentially the best strategy for developing the uniqueness of their 'past cities'. If the economic power of a contemporary city – a city in the global network economy – lies in its ability to focus in one place and time many threads, connections and flows, one of which lies at the level of personal relations and sentiments, then is it not the most important clue as to how we should proceed? Especially if it is true that 'the City exists mainly in the imagination'. The weakness of the City, the weakness of the urban community, comes from the same source as its strength – the flows. Flows that rinse capital and people out of the City. Flows that do not give roots.

Globalisation presents the peripheral and semi-peripheral countries with an evil alternative which has been repeatedly highlighted by Jadwiga

Staniszkis; worse than being exploited, for the cities of these countries, is to remain non-exploited – left outside the global market. The same remark also applies to cities that either become part of the global streams, with all their consequences, or are excluded from them. But is this really the only alternative that exists?

CITY MANAGEMENT   II.VI
Managerial Governance against 'the Local Community'

Managing a city is naturally an extremely complex task – after all, the city itself is a strange, heterogeneous creation that escapes definition. However, each management is based on a methodology, and above all has certain initial assumptions, which are defined by priorities and objectives. Therefore, we can talk about certain models of cities: models of city management and urban space. Suppose that there are only two models; one of which details the management of experts, based on professional, 'rationalised' knowledge – management to a certain extent authoritarian, which treats the city as a kind of enterprise – and the second based on a bottom-up mechanism of 'folk' and strictly democratic-communal management. With the latter I mean 'the local community', because the strong social ties that constitute a community may only be found in neighbouring units. The problem in describing a city that is managed 'communally' lies in the fact that we still do not deal with an urban community, but only with a set of local communities.

Divisions between managerial and 'communal' governance run across the distinctions to which we were accustomed until recently. 'Expert' governance – or better, management – was dominant in both the U.S. and the Soviet bloc countries. Today, the two poles – the two model cities to be considered, reflecting contemporary methods of urban space management – lie entirely outside the existing central areas of the world: they are Singapore in Asia and Porto Alegre in South America (similarly managerial is the governance of Dubai, but there we are dealing primarily with an authoritarian – however enlightened – ruler, therefore Singapore seems to be a better, more interesting example). Singapore, the City-State, in a sense resembles the Italian cities of the Renaissance period or the ancient Greek Polis (but is, however, more like Sparta than any other ancient Greek polis – Sparta was a xenophobic city, while others were surprisingly cosmopolitan).[27] Porto Alegre in turn is also a case irresistibly associated with the Greek model of the city. Porto Alegre, however, with its 'participatory budget' is far closer to Athens and a democratic, egalitarian community. These two cities – two models and two ideas – may reflect the two poles of thinking about city management.

Of course, in addition to these models there is a huge spectrum of different intermediate models, where expert management mixes with social participation. Even in these two cities – which are extremes – there are traces of footprints that lead elsewhere. But if we take these two cities as the 'purest' examples of two (contradictory?) ideologies, then we can ask whether or not they really are so different from each other. After all, both refer in a direct way to the Greek origins of cities as political communities. So maybe these cities are two sides of the same coin? Singapore is officially a parliamentary republic. In fact, despite the existence of a formal opposition, the People's Action Party has ruled the country quite a lot since the creation of local government in 1959.

With less than five million inhabitants, and stable economic growth (despite the famous 'Asian crisis' in 1997), Singapore has one of the highest standards of living in Asia. In other words – it is a paradise on Earth. What is so unusual about this City-State is its clear determination to survive and to succeed. Managerial governance of this creature began immediately after it become independent in 1961, and in a manner rather typical of companies (or clubs) the Dutch economist Dr Albert Winsemius was recruited to work as economic advisor in Singapore, remaining there until his retirement in 1984. He is greatly responsible for its effective – as it turned out – strategy for development. The ruling party in the City-State was considered the beginning of a Socialist party but has always been characterised by pragmatism – it combined support for big state construction programs with incentives for foreign investors. Singapore has never been a minimal state. It has been – and still is – known for actively interfering in economic processes, in terms of supporting and placing particular businesses, but these actions have always based on the pursuit of the City's material success as a whole. And it seems that this success has been achieved: not only is Singapore the 22nd richest country in the world but it also has the highest standard of living in Asia (according to the *The Economist*). This pragmatic development of the city is probably a result of its geographical location – lying on an island, Singapore has been forced into a rational management of its space and resources. Also, a denser population seems to be preferred – Singapore is developing an Asian version of the compact city. Such cities are characterised by the low cost, high-intensity development of technical infrastructures and amenities such as electricity, gas and water (where the low cost is in part due to low transport costs). Singapore's inhabitants have everything 'close', but to me the most important thing is the vision that has guided its government – and certainly the people – since the inception of the City-State. If the state exists primarily in the imagination, then the people of Singapore must share the same vision and they must believe in it very strongly. In Singapore, social inequalities – as in other cities managing a neoliberal regime – are rising, but the city is maintained by a conscious policy of immigration, resulting in a population shift towards highly skilled professionals, with a very small increase of the so-called 'underclass'. Thus, despite the widening gap between the richest citizens and the poorest residents of Singapore, the population of this first group is growing faster than the other.[28]

Porto Alegre is in many ways a city to which Singapore cannot be compared. Just one of many big cities in Brazil, it has 'only' 1.3 million inhabitants with an incomparably smaller budget (about $700 million, while Singapore's budget is around $30 billion) and, above all, is not a City-State. However, Porto Alegre has the highest standard of living in Brazil, and is the only city in Brazil on the list of so-called 'World Winning Cities' prepared by one of the largest real estate companies in the world, Jones Lang LaSalle, which in some way entitles this city to a comparison with Singapore. When a bloc of left-wing parties came to power in 1989, Porto Alegre was not poor. However, it was characterised by great social inequalities: almost one third of the population occupied substandard housing; that is – strictly speaking – lived in shantytowns, often without running water or a sewage system. In 1985, the Congress UAMPA (União das Associações de Moradores de Porto Alegre – Union of Associations of Neighbouring in Porto Alegre) called for the creation of mechanisms for public participation in determining priorities for budget spending in the city, but no one knew exactly what these mechanisms would look like.[29] In the end, a model consisting of a common share of people was developed – people as individuals and as representatives of major social forces – in setting budget priorities. These kinds of 'popular assembly' are held once a year (in March) throughout individual districts. In addition to the general decisions about the allocation of the budget, representatives are elected for a kind of audit committee to examine the uses and effects of the budget expenditure for the past year.[30] Over several decades of operation, Porto Alegre has become a symbol of success in democratic urban governance; its model for drawing up budgets has been adopted by more than 170 other cities in Brazil and it is widely discussed around the world. Social inequalities have been minimised, while the city has become more egalitarian and secure.

As you can see, despite their operational differences, the systems for city management in Porto Alegre and Singapore share one – very important – feature. Both cities exist in a kind of 'heightened alert' – a continuous process of prioritisation, and continuous monitoring of the effects of earlier assumptions. As Jadwiga Staniszkis would put it, both these cities are still inventing themselves anew.

Between Singapore and Porto Alegre there are other models of the city. Some of them – like other cities in Brazil and some in India – are closer to Porto Alegre, while the majority, especially European cities (due to the dominance of Enlightenment, rationalist discourses), are closer to the neoliberal aspects of Singapore. This may sound strange but whether or not countries are 'fully democratic', managerial city management was and still is the most popular model. Generally speaking, managerial governance consists of the primacy of technocrats, seemingly reasonable goals and rationalised methods. But we know (not just from Foucault) that decision making is always based on these or other priorities. There is no 'neutral power'; power always represents someone's interests at the cost of another's. A good example of the seemingly rationalised process of change in modern (European or American) cities is gentrification.

At first glance, it consists of the revitalisation of neglected areas; the poor, to use a cliché, deprived areas. These neglected – but potentially attractive – areas sooner or later become objects of interest to developers. For if the current price of land is much lower than the price that could potentially be obtained for certain plots, the capitalist profit maximisation mechanism will inevitably lead to the transformation of these district from 'useless' (in the capitalist sense) into 'useful'. According to the Rental Gap Theory, neglected neighbourhoods that – because of their location or exceptional qualities (historic, scenic, sentimental, etc.) – are attractive to investors, are also subject to market pressure. But developers, even in consortiums, are often too weak and too afraid to take on the challenge of revitalisation. As in the cases of the London and Belfast docks, there arises a so-called public-private partnership that creates a protective umbrella for private capital. The only – but crucial – problem is the people living there. They are often poor, often socially pathological – sometimes criminal – elements of society. So the slow process of pushing these people out of their neighbourhood begins. This is done through the purchase of land and housing, as well as changes in local planning regulations with which these people are unable to cope. Public-private partnerships not only create an umbrella over the institutional changes that occur but also, through their 'public' element – indeed, often due to public consultations (as required by law) – produce a type of moral umbrella that justifies and soothes the actions of developers. Neoliberal regimes, which are currently the most common method of urban management, commit the municipal administration to defending and representing the developer. Here a diabolical element of managerial governance emerges, incorporating various programs for the revitalisation of neglected urban areas, which effects a delicate social lobotomy – it cuts people off from the places that they know and where they are used to living, and forces them to move. The neoliberal approach differs from classical liberalism in that we are not dealing with a clean market game, but with an interaction of administrations and politicians with capital. The differences relate to the interpretation of the purposes of neoliberalism – the official goal is simply to extend the sphere of the free market (with a strong share of the state) in order to increase economic efficiency and enhance capital accumulation. However, David Harvey argues that the real target of this ideology is simply to restore the position of the higher social classes.[31] Harvey, using the classical method of inquiry, asks whom neoliberalism really is serving – who benefits and who loses. The answer he gives is this: the very rich gain and everyone else loses. Progressive income disparities and social stratification in countries where neoliberalism is the dominant ideology (primarily in the U.S. but similarly in Russia, and even Poland) seem to confirm Harvey's thesis. His diagnosis will also be useful in describing the changes that are managed by the city of a neoliberal regime.

Managerial governance – which today is almost synonymous with a neoliberal regime – is nothing other than the defense and empowerment of groups that have a strong and privileged position in society, at the expense of all others. The idea of revitalising 'dead' urban space is, after all, worthy of support – the only problem is that while this revitalisation restores an excluded area to the city, it 'pushes' disadvantaged groups farther beyond the boundaries of a healthy city. The revitalisation of urban space in the majority of cases, therefore, concerns only a part of the urban question –

that which relates to space and the economy – and completely ignores social problems. The ultimate goal is to push the revitalisation of disadvantaged areas and groups outside the administrative boundaries of the city. Here we see the fundamental difference between 'dirty' managerial governance and the management style in Singapore. 'Dirty' managerial governance (not all of them are, of course) is a cynical use of the masks of 'common good', 'global competition', 'protecting the most vulnerable' and – above all – 'freedom', in order to protect and promote the strong, rich and privileged. Singapore does not use a mask but openly carries a 'war' policy of building the city's strength, making it a city of full and informed participation for its citizens. Also, pushing the poor outside the city of Singapore would be quite difficult, because 'outside' of the borders there is 'nothing'. There is no political entity that would be able to adopt the unwanted and they would be forced into emigration.

One might ask – how is it possible that an elite-oriented management can be applied in cities where the authorities have come from a democratic election? Does this happen because the most privileged layers are the majority? It seems that in the case of managerial governance, we are in fact dealing with multi-story neoliberal lies (There Is No Alternative – 'TINA') and the myth of a 'rational future'. Managerial governance, as every elitist system, is premised on the people's belief that if someone is successful, they will somehow confer the miraculous power of this success onto the community. However, if managerial governance is so common everywhere and in all systems, maybe there actually is *no alternative*. Besides, what is wrong with the fact that cities are managed by people according to their best knowledge – people who are filled with concern for the fate of future generations and wish to ensure a bright future for the city?

There are two arguments against this – one technical and one political. The technical argument applies to the mythologisation 'rational decisions'. As noted above, every decision – every normative system – is based on certain axioms and priorities; even if we assume that specific technical solutions leading to specific targets can be left to the technocrats, discussion is still needed to decide on these targets. The discussion of what kind of city we want is a debate which, at their own level of competence, each inhabitant of the city may partake in – as shown by the successful experiment of Porto Alegre. Other social experiments show that such 'collective wisdom' often brings better solutions than those devised by even the best experts, because the collective unit has the capability to look widely and through multiple perspectives while the lone expert has only experience to his advantage. Of course, I do not wish to say that experts are useless, but their task should not rely only on providing the necessary professional knowledge and partaking in the 'management decision making process'.

The second argument against managerial governance is political – or social; it concerns the social compaction of the city, which is threatened by a managerial-neoliberal regime. Even in Singapore, in which the 'war' aspect of urban governance seems to me more prevalent than the managerial, society is stratifying. Maybe not very much but it is still happening. When writing about the 'war' aspect of management, I mean – in part – regimes that challenge the egoistical purposes of the higher social classes in the name of a 'common good'. As I indicated, a probable cause of this mutation of Singapore's managerial governance is the fact that one cannot escape from the city to the 'outside', and this internal pressure – forcing all the residents to live together – has led to the existence of some kind of municipal community.

Today, both the right (obviously) and the left (surprisingly) are attacking the idea of full inclusion for all excluded groups as unrealistic and even harmful. However, I am going to remain a supporter of an old idiom – one person is worth as much to me as the whole world. And that is why I will not agree on an incoherent system for urban communities. There are also practical reasons for this view – each excluded group (especially systemically excluded) is aggressive and dangerous for the 'rest'. It is cheaper (in terms of social costs) to seek to integrate rather than face the danger of revolt. The French riots in 2005 show how this might look in practice – the social and spatial exclusion of large social groups results in violence. Always and everywhere. Which is precisely why the aforementioned Singapore is an example of how social engineering – aimed at creating a capable city-enterprise, with satisfied and well paid citizen-employees – is particularly efficient. If a city must, however, be a political entity capable of protecting its citizens, and an alternative to the Empire, then it must give up elite management practices and the potential for an entire urban community. The examples of Singapore and Porto Alegre show that the restoration of the city as a political community may be effected in different ways. Intensified democracy, despite provoking an obvious sympathy, seems somehow incomplete. Logically, an appropriate method of managing the city – a method that actually creates Polis – should be found somewhere between the Singapore and Porto Alegre models. But what is beyond this dichotomy?

II.VII   'Dispersed' Power against 'Real' Power

There is, in contemporary political thought, a strong philosophical – or sociological – tendency to write about power structures only in context, and to think of power as a fuzzy, anonymous network. Discussions of personified, 'held-by-a-person' power seem increasingly obsolete. In fact, they do not even describe reality. After Foucault, we can no longer see government as usual. However, I have the impression that in dredging deeper and deeper, is searching for a new lining to reality, we lose something – are missing something. Authority has become so fragmented and volatile that any rebellion against it now seems like a silly fight with a windmill. Power has become invisible and more powerful than ever. Trapped in its structures, we lose the possibility of revolt. Dispersed power – the power of a capillary, filled all the time – becomes totalitarian power, present in the public sphere and appropriating the private sphere. The latter ceases to exist.

In modern criticisms of cities, one of the first things to be mentioned is usually the disappearance of public spaces. As discussed in previous chapters, I consider this process to be negligible. It does not evoke any emotion in me, because public spaces have no significance for the city today. They lost their political significance, and today they exist in closing cinemas. Of course, public space is still a space in which to meet different people, but the struggle for public space as such is like powdering a corpse. More worrying are the changes in the private sphere. If the disappearance of public spaces, and their replacement with commercial spaces, is a simple consequence of the conversion of the Citizen into the Citizen-Consumer and the disappearance of politics from daily life, then the growth of private space in the city is a type of cancer that is devouring the very essence of urbanity.

Public (but not political) spaces do not differ significantly from commercial spaces. However, one cannot just go into a private space. So if the city is a

Machine of Exchange, commercial spaces have a right to existence; we may not like them, we may believe that they are vulgar, but they are – and always have been – a part of the city and urbanity. Privatised spaces were a part of historic cities, but as alien, external ulcers. Urbanity is a flow. Private parts block this movement – and I refer here to the classical Nolli's map of Rome, which shows precisely the relationship between private and public spaces. Certain private spaces – homes, apartments, etc. – are an obvious part of an approved urban fabric but others, such as castles, parks and closed areas, are not. Such private spaces in contemporary cities are not the intimate spaces of freedom. They are oppression, founded on the separation of what is 'better' from what is 'worse' – only to keep the 'better' under close observation and prevent it from morphing, so that it cannot be 'broken'. Regulations in force at closed estates, shopping malls and office complexes arranged in the shape of fortresses are characteristic of Foucault's model of disciplinary power. If we are amused and frightened by the regulations to which the inhabitants of the Soviet house-communes were subjected, and if we recognise that interference with the privacy of prisoners is one of the worst aspects of a prison sentence, then surely the regulation of privatised spaces, coupled with constant CCTV surveillance of the 'public', should also raise our opposition? The fact that it does not shows how much we have let these power structures – against which we feel completely helpless, and therefore allow ourselves to support – enter into our private lives. And I certainly do not think that this loss of freedom is the worst. Any adjustment to some extent restricts freedom. Worse is, firstly, the fact that those agreeing with the anonymity and blurring (and thus a kind of sublimation and 'spiritisation') of power do not try to take over and appropriate this power. Secondly, it is a frightening acceptance of the fact that the private has become postpolitical.

The worst thing about the devouring of our private lives by the postpolitical machine is the loss of intimate relationships. The Me-You relationship, which is crucial for the construction of any community, has disappeared. Today there is a Me-System-You relationship. The system may take the form of law, it may be political correctness – about which Žižek writes – and it may be an archaic convention that governs the ordinary rules of a housing estate. Its function is always the same: to disrupt the intimate, personal, unique and authentic Me-You relationship.

I have a great fondness for Finland and the Finnish. One of the reasons why I tend to regard this nation so highly is the respect which the Finns (and their

State) have for everyone. The genesis of this feature is easy to understand in terms of their culture – the Finns are not the largest of populations, while the climate and difficult living conditions sometimes made life extremely tough. A need for cooperation evolved into a respect and concern for each person which you can see in everyday life (for example, in the education system). It was also seen during the Second World War, when the Finns fought against the Soviet Union. Russian soldiers were sent to their deaths in the tens of thousands (the famous, and then used with relish 'diagnosis by battle'), while the Finns tried to face them in small groups. The Soviet penchant for the masses (like the body) was not a purely Soviet, but rather a Byzantine belief that somewhere there is an absolute ruler, and was present first in Russian, then Soviet ("we say – the party, and implicitly – Lenin"[32]), and again in Russian society today. This Byzantinism is rooted in monotheistic religion; Christianity. Alain de Benoist – not without reason – sees monotheism at the core of any European totalitarianism. Monotheism, by definition, sees God as a transcendent legislator. Here we come to a problem that has interested me for some time. Catholicism inherently possesses the seed of revolution and, looking at the Church's mainstream, Catholicism is not at all as obviously totalitarian as we might think. In addition to Christianity, this 'immanentism' is very strongly present in Chinese culture. As John King Fairbank wrote: "Ancient Chinese people did not know [...] the myths of creation or creator, the legislature of the heavens, the first cause or even the Big Bang. [...] This view opposes the tendency rooted anywhere else in the world – the establishment of the existence of supernatural deities."[33]

How am I to reconcile what I have written with Chinese communism? How to reconcile this with the earlier Empire? Not only are external forces totalitarian, internal relationships and social rules not founded anywhere 'outside' society can also be devastating to the individual. However, these 'internal' regulations have one great advantage over the 'external' – they are flexible and changeable. As Jadwiga Staniszkis put it in *Globalisation's Authority*, China is a culture that has the power to manipulate itself.[34] This strength comes precisely from the rejection of external legislature; the rejection of transcendence. Of course, I am not forgetting the labour camps, political prisoners, Tibet or Tiananmen Square, but I can hardly escape the impression that the 'real China' is different. That its people can be as brutal and cruel as any other nation, but have in fact never been particularly belligerent or aggressive towards their neighbours. Rather, China was overrun by the Mongols and it was more the Japanese than they who provoked the war. So when thinking about freedom, about a person and not the masses, I see not only Finland but also, completely paradoxically as it would seem, China. Freedom may be limited because of both God and the neighbour. However, the neighbour may die or be tamed, while God takes our freedom by the mere fact of being God.

The Me-You relationship (or I-Thou, according to Martin Buber) is the key to liberation. In the words of Emmanuel Levinas: "Beginning with Plato, the social ideal will be sought for in an ideal of fusion [...] the collectivity that says 'we', that, turned toward the intelligible sun, toward the truth, feels the other at its side and not in front of itself. [...] Against this collectivity of the side-by-side, I have tried to oppose the 'I-you' collectivity [...] not a participation in a third term, whether this term be a person, a truth, a work, or a profession. It is a collectivity that is not a communion. It is the face-to-face without intermediary."[35] Fuzzy, dissipated power, hidden in the structures and systems, is still – perhaps more so than before – the power of the divine, the transcendent. An authority which is not produced but can only be passively received. So if we want to look for the City as a political community, we should first try to grasp the power in its concrete, real-time dimension. We need to somehow push through the postpolitical machinery regulating our privacy in order to understand and then harness the power of the broad, fuzzy, public sphere. In the cases to which I have referred (Singapore and Porto Alegre) the urban communities have, to some extent, self-control. So can we say that it does not matter whether the power is exercised by the community, who is involved in an ongoing process of control and management, or whether it is sufficient that the community delegates its powers, giving selected, personified rulers its trust? Of course it matters. But let us start by saying that neither the models of Porto Alegre nor Singapore represent a new model of Polis. The Me-You relationship is lost because, in any modern city, this relationship is too fragile and intimate to be able, without adequate construction, to become the core of the political system of the City. Therefore, the search for a foundation for Polis should begin by determining the conditions under which the Me-You relationship can arise and go beyond the most intimate human relationships. As I have said, this relationship is very fragile. It seems impossible that it can exist anywhere outside a strictly private relationship. One would think that if it can, then you could look for clues in the institutional mind, or even in far-left anarchists. However, I would suggest a different path – a completely different direction. I would like to find forms for the Me-You relationship within an institution which was a great success, and I am not the only one who finds this institution fascinating. This institution is the Catholic Church.

Catholicism, in its deepest belief, contains the seeds of revolution in comparison with which all the leftist projects are mere child's play. The kernel of the Catholic revolution lies in the rejection of Law by Jesus. So if one is looking for a way to eliminate the system from the Me-System-You relationship, then he seems to be a good guide. Jesus challenged the rules – and therefore something that is transcendent to man – and instead proposed a love that sets the rules between all people who form relationships with each other, not just intimate relationships. Speaking of love, instead of the Law, love must be understood very broadly – just as in any sincere relationships between people. Any such relationship is different, each of which is 'local'. There is no possibility – I have no doubt about it – of a 'direct' Me-You relationship. There must always be something through which we enter into a relationship – some kind of language. The Law system, however, is a language – a medium – which does not belong to us. It is external to us but it is not neutral, it always belongs to 'someone' else. Using it, we let a stranger – not necessarily friendly to us, after all – become 'the third party'. With truly intimate relationships, people can build their own media, create their own intimate language, and this trail should be our primary lead. There are numerous cases of couples where the partners have come from other cultures and other languages, and it is not so rare to find that the language they speak among themselves is really their own private language – built, of course, on the basis of their mother tongues, but essentially a language that is different, separate. I have stated several times over that the Me-You relationship is fragile. It is local, and in this locality lies both its strength and a great weakness. The particularity of this relationship vividly recalls the particularity of City as a political idea, about which Pierre Manent wrote. The City solves its problems, manages them in a specific time and place, under certain conditions. The City does not lay claim to universality. Similarly, the Me-You relationship is enclosed within the parties – it does not claim to be the universal relation, and is not imperial. So can this particularity in some way be strengthened?

St. Paul, in creating a church, at the same time knocked the teeth out of the Revolution of Jesus. The 'establishment of universalism', which pleases Badiou so, was a defeat rather than a victory, but still in Christianity, and especially Catholicism, these seeds of the revolution remain. This can best be seen in some of the sacraments – such as the sacrament of marriage, which spouses provide to each other; God, the priest and other people are all just witnesses. What is important is what happens within the community of two people. Similarly, you can see a seed of the Revolution of Jesus in the sacrament of penance. We are dealing here with an intimate encounter between the wicked and the righteous (yes, acting as a representative of God), in which the sinner is confronted with the law, the Rule, but through a Person (God or priest, it does not matter), and it is from this intimate relationship that the forgiveness of sin follows. After all, Jesus had set this relationship as follows: "if you forgive people's sins, they are forgiven. If you retain people's sins, they are retained." These seeds of Revolution, which are fixed in Catholicism, are still a fresh call for the rejection of the Law and the meeting of a Person. How important is this revolution, testify the contemporary explorations by the new left, which – as Agata Bielik-Robson accuses Žižek – negates the individual human being and his happiness, rejecting a person as liberal-capitalist ballast?[36] Every ideology is a Law, and the Law violates and kills people. It does not matter whose Law it is – whether capitalist, fascist or Bolshevik – Law is always a source of violence, a source of suffering. The revolution of Jesus is still awaiting its completion. The Church of St. Paul was afraid of it (though it retained the seed), they were afraid of everyone who disagreed with the Church and fought against it – though they did try to pursue some fragments of this revolution. So the true revolution of Jesus is still ahead of us. Looking for the foundations of Polis, we will inevitably have to measure ourselves against it – one way or another.

Think back to the urban models considered earlier: it seems clear that the model of Porto Alegre is much closer to maintaining a dialogical relationship than the authoritarian Singapore model – however, it may not always be so. As argued by Edward F. Greaves, "in some spatial-institutional contexts, the participatory governance (a system in which social organisations are included by the authority – in this case local – in the structure of city management) may be an instrument for disciplining the realm of the 'civic'." That is, participating in authority may serve to change or maintain the existing hegemony. When power is used for the purpose of amendment, the mechanism of participation acts as a catalyst which gives social organisations influence over (and even the ability to take over) local authorities and also strengthens existing social networks. Conversely, when a local authority wishes to maintain the existing social and political hegemony, participation takes place only under certain conditions and its aim is to weaken and break down independent social movements. The Porto Alegre model works with success only in conditions guaranteed by the real impact of participating in the management of residents on the shape and future of the city, and an acceptance of the limitations of this process. This condition also implies that the city has a substantial level of autonomy (in terms of finance and management) from the state. At this point, the Porto Alegre model is nearing the Singapore model. Still, these two examples leave us a little unsatisfied. Both are tainted with transcendent power – power which incapacitates. Additionally, the Porto Alegre model creates strong neighbourhoods but not a strong city as a whole. Perhaps there is no other authority. Perhaps we cannot even conceive another authority. But maybe somewhere at the root of our thoughts about the society, we accept an axiom which deprives us of the chance to find another model of inherent power.

Plug-in Citizen as a Prerequisite for the Resurrection of Polis II.VIII
Polis as a Defense and Liberation

I described the crisis of the City as a disappearance of the political community. As a slow disappearance of all communities and a loss of the City's capability for self-management. As the transformation of the City from a political idea, an autonomous entity, into a space colonised by beings rooted 'elsewhere'. Ultimately, as a loss of strength by the City and of the desire to protect its citizens. This crisis is combined, of course, with the processes of globalisation, and the disappearance of hierarchical systems in favour of network systems. Networking is considered to be a chance for the future, for the liberation of people from the oppression of hierarchical and centralised power. Anarchist – and perhaps, with time, also Communist – ideologies sometimes appear to see networking technology as something that has introduced their ideals through the back door. I could probably agree with this opinion, were it not for a little 'but'. But – what about the person? When living in a city, do they always work for some global (or local, but dependent on global markets and banks) company? Considering the spatial, political and social structures of cities in the data stream, where we have millions of people before our eyes, we lose sight of the person. If they appear anywhere it is in a work of art rather than in the work of practising scientists and planners. An individual person has ceased to be important in the global world of flows and networks. However, if you want to restore Polis as the axis of the political community, then it is the person, the 'citizen' (but not in the Greek, the Enlightenment nor the modern sense – so a new kind of citizen or, as I try to describe it, a 'Plug-in Citizen') who must stand at the centre of our interest.

It is time to put my cards on the table. This book is founded on the belief that neither ideas nor ideologies are important if you ignore the life and happiness of an individual. 'Truth' and 'good' are morally suspect, if they cause someone to suffer. One of this book's inspirations dates back to the 'Oration of the

Dignity of Man' by Picco della Mirandola: "I do not designate you, Adam, neither a specific seat, nor a face, nor do I give you any specific function, so that any seat, any face or any feature you desire, you may possess in accordance to your wishes and your will. The nature of all other beings has been determined and included in the limits we set. But you, unfettered by any restrictions, I give into your own hands, so that by your nature you identify yourself. According to your will. [...] I put you in the middle of the world, the more easily that you can observe everything that is happening in the world. I have made you neither heavenly creature, nor earthly, neither mortal nor immortal, so you as a free and worthy creator and sculptor of yourself can choose the shape that you want. You will be able to roll up and degenerate to the level of animals and you will be able to revive your spirit and strength to rise to the rank of divine beings."[37] It is up to us, the people, who we become and the kind of world in which we live. Networking – in its simplest form, the individual point of view – is usually treated as a great opportunity to communicate directly and associate with the global network: the Internet. Everyone who works (or at least corresponds) with people throughout the world realises that this network can ignore geographical location, and brings people who use the web into a single place. The fact that this 'place' exists in a virtual space does not matter. Communication is done within it, so in that sense it is completely real.

This fantastic opportunity, the 'compression' of space, discharges it at one point, causing us to lose sight of the negative aspects of such a 'universal' communication and networking system. While we receive dozens, sometimes hundreds of emails each day (worth reading and sometimes even worth responding), and have scores of web messenger and social media contacts, people are not really using the power of this network. The strength of the network is only potential power; I repeat: 'being' kills potentiality. Life is a desperate loss of opportunities. Instead of the potential existence of infinite dimensions, we fill our lives with one in particular. Are we sure that it is the best one possible? From this point of view, networking both strengthens and weakens us. We have a limited amount of time, and trying to maintain a vast network makes it 'blurred'. However, this issue – which affects individuals – does not apply to larger organisations. This is a crucial difference: networking strengthens groups, but weakens individual human beings. In this sense, networking adds nothing new to the classical mechanics of social relations. The crowd always existed beyond the individual being of a person. The only difference – the non-hierarchical nature of the network – actually works against the individual, and prevents their location in the site hierarchy and a significant gain of influence on reality. By definition, networking prevents the impact of the individual. Of course, in reality, impacts are made but they are much smaller than in a hierarchical system – what a paradox! Institutions that use the network may grow – hiring new employees, devouring one another, entering into alliances. There is obviously some difficulty in managing large, global organisms, but it is possible. Giants are becoming stronger. A human being is only one. A person is weak in their singleness. If they had a chance at a local level, if they still had the illusion of their importance in a national dimension, then the global dimension of the network takes away their illusions: "the individual is nonsense, the individual is zero."[38] Today, this sentiment is truer than ever.

The global corporations of the world benefit from the network and the 'ordinary people' are becoming weaker; blurred and confused. Meanwhile, trying to retain our individual identities and meanings, we are doing two things: either we create a network, a group, by ceding our individuality in order to build ourselves into a larger whole – and we have done this throughout the pre-Internet era – or we limit our bonds within a network to a few, which we can control, and thus try to retain our autonomy and uniqueness. Both these ways of functioning in a globalised world have a desperate taste of desertion. If we dissolve into a group then our only freedom lies in the fact that we may choose one group over another. However, the group's strength depends on the loyalty of its members, so it is irrelevant whether it is a religious or counter-cultural group – very strong, mafia-like sectarian ties are at play. Fleeing from a global loss of meaning, we remain in bondage. Limiting our social activity to a few friends is a pure desertion from the global world. Perhaps we could survive, if we were vigilant and well-hidden from the world. In the latter case we give up entirely our attempts to influence the world, and in the former we do so through other groups. Yes – they strengthen our chances in the world, but they weaken us as autonomous individuals. Because network – even when created with the best intentions – is a strong force which is composed of individuals. Even more painful is the fact that networks inherently contain nodes in which each individual is a replaceable item, and this is causing our loss of meaning and subjectivity. The problem is then the fact that networks eventually force weakness upon individuals. The bigger and stronger the network, the weaker we become – though at first glance the opposite seems to be the case. This is, in my opinion, the most serious challenge that we face in a Global World.

Networking is one of the most popular hype-words. We have network society (Castells) and global cities linked in a network (Sassen, Taylor). The global network, which is the Internet, I have already mentioned. Describing the world in terms of its networks is appealing, and indeed – if we are to understand the contemporary world – quite effective. However, the subjective, 'grass roots' perspective – let's call it 'sociological' – can also tell us something interesting about the world in which we live. So instead of considering the links in the network, I would prefer a moment to consider the nodes in themselves, and the individuals moving between them.

I noticed 'pointuality' in our experience of the world for the first time while using the metro system in Paris. In 1991, I had the opportunity to move around the city this way and I felt quite strongly that while on a city tour by subway it does not exist as a continuous structure – it exists as a series of areas suddenly appearing around the metro. Of course, all of these points are linked in a network, but for my existential experience those links do not matter. The time when I am between the different nodes of a network is time wasted. It is dead time. Nodes are irrelevant; the relationships between them are not. From the user's point of view, the network is simply significant points separated by nothingness. That is why the reality of the Internet is so compelling and fascinating – because it compresses this space, bringing together at one point people who are in contact.

The existence of a person in a 'pre-network' society was limited by their mobility. But at that time people were still building a network of links with the outside world – family, clan, friendship, etc. This network was hierarchical and – you might say – organic. When moving into an area on foot, we can at any time come into physical contact with the reality that surrounds us, but by getting into a bus or car (not to mention a plane) we lose this contact. To simplify the problem, we can say that our contact with the surrounding world depends on the intensity and the 'depth' of our relationships with each other, and on the time that we devote to these relationships. When a person's mobility is limited, their chance to connect and engage with the environment is obviously greater. Networked society, which increases mobility, makes it difficult for them to connect to their surroundings, and leads to a 'blurred' being. There is a Hindu story which tells that the soul of a human being cannot keep up with them flying on a plane. We must therefore wait for the soul. When traveling, whether by plane or train – especially outside the boundaries of our language (and even more so when traveling outside our alphabet) – we lose the opportunity to have a relationship with the world at all. Rather, we are forced to close in on ourselves. To autism. Freedom and ease of contact through the Internet is often illusory – how easy it is to lose an identity, to break a relationship.

The networking of the global world is tearing off our 'natural roots', which usually grow into the surrounding world. We become infirm and lonely. But it's not necessarily so. There are still nodes between which we move. In these nodes, we refer mostly to contact with the world (or rather – perhaps more importantly – people). Sometimes quite intensely. The only thing we have to learn is how to grow into our 'roots' through nothingness. Global, network-based 'fuzzy' power rules the world and makes a person become confused and weak – a fragmented network of connections and relationships. With a lack of strong and durable bonds to social causes, in a confrontation with global institutions a person has absolutely no chance. The processes of globalisation, which increase the power of supranational institutions, radically diminish the forces of the individual. So apparently, the solution to the problem of globalisation should be some kind of network citizenship – to strengthen and adapt to current trends. In this conception of citizenship, networks are consistent with both the concept of citizenship of the city, and the binding of a person's fate to the corporation (or other organisation) and use of its internal systems of social security and services.

The fundamental issue seems to be human – of human being. A working hypothesis, contained in the term Plug-in Citizen, is the concept of strong structures which exist in some sense independently of the citizens. People, by nature, have access to these structures. However, human beings do not exist as a complete network – but only in 'flashes'. They appear in certain parts of an existing network with their whole being, and are thus charged by the power of the structure into which they plug themselves. It is this structure which gives a human being the strength that an individual is missing. There are certain ideas emerging, such as Bruno Frey's, which suggest an even stronger 'fragmentation' of nationality and the granting of people who have dual (or multiple) nationality partial electoral rights – for example, half of the vote in each of the two countries in which they are a citizen.[39]

Characteristically, however, the fact that the political significance of citizenship is being published in texts, and presented in ideas, is becoming less relevant. In fact, this path leads to the decline of the citizen as a political entity, and causes the disappearance of policy and weakens the importance of politics as a counterbalance to market forces. A person does not grow as a corporation. They are unable to locate the entire network; lack the forces, resources, time. A person is a single being-point with limited resources and possibilities within the existence of the network. So it seems that there is an urgent need to rethink the very essence of the concept of people as a part of the political system. Moreover, there is a need for a radical reconstruction of the political system, to remake it into a strong and efficient global institution. An institution for the exercise of power. If we are talking about a democratic system, we are talking about self-power of the people over themselves – Mankind. The restoration of control over one's own human being. We are talking not only about the political system – we are talking about the takeover of power by the people through biopolitics, but I will return to this in later chapters.

The aforementioned Bruno Frey is the author of the concept of COM (Citizenship: Organisational and Marginal), which would allow free choice in belonging to any organisation, group or corporation. We would be able to choose between being British, European, Catholic or a Citizen of Nike. There are also ideas relating to citizenship within smaller territorial units – a region (such as Cornwall, the Highlands, or Greater Poland) and a city. The tendency to deconstruct the nation-state is certainly understandable – the degree of a citizen's identification with their country, not only in Britain and Poland, is decreasing rather than increasing. The problem, however, concerns the very foundation of the importance of being a citizen. A citizen is someone who has responsibilities to the state (let us stick for a moment to the meaning of citizenship as understood in the nineteenth and twentieth centuries), and complies with the law, pays taxes, and has an obligation of loyalty and even to defend. Citizens also have privileges. They have the care of the state in their hands, in terms of both the political (a citizen has the right to influence the choice of state authorities, and for the state to protect the rights of its citizen while they reside under another law) and in terms of social pressures (the European welfare state surrounds its citizens with the comprehensive care of disease, injury and old age, providing them with assistance in difficult and unexpected situations). The nature of citizenship can therefore be determined as a contract between state and citizen. A contract which, in certain cases, can be broken – a state may persecute its citizens, either all or just some groups, and the citizen can escape under the protection of another country, seeking political asylum.

Political asylum is in fact an interesting example of the loss of meaning of 'the political'. It is increasingly difficult to find because of the lack of political rights in one's country. On this basis, one billion Chinese people could ask for political asylum because of a lack of satisfaction with their political rights in China. So if political asylum is granted, it only concerns specific examples of life-threatening, severe persecution. This would then be the biological dimension of citizenship, which I mentioned at the beginning of this book. But I say frankly: political asylum is of political importance, rather than at the level of struggle and rivalry between state organisms. If a country accepts refugees from another country, and is doing so primarily to 'condemn' another country in the international arena in order to demonstrate its superiority, then there is less concern for human rights and more 'civilised' legislation. Political asylum is often a cynical instrument used by the state for its own purposes, and not a proof of citizenship and the political importance of its international recognition. So I repeat again: the key is to find a formula for a post-citizen existence. One that would give people roots, security and liberation.

Let me now describe three occurrences, which may seem unrelated to each other or to the contents of this chapter. In the first scene we see a British policeman, Gary Pettengella, who has received the Guardian Angel medal from the hands of the Lithuanian president, and was recognised by Lithuanian television as Personality of the Year 2006 and by the people of Norfolk as Policeman of the Year. What can that nice officer have done? He saw within the uneducated Lithuanian crowds coming to work in Norfolk – unfamiliar with the English language or regulations – citizens. Not 'people' but just citizens. European Union citizens; legal residents in the UK who should be assisted in becoming – as far as possible – parts of the social and economic System of the Isles. He not only saw them – using the opportunities afforded by being part of the state machine – but he actually helped these people to settle in Britain. First, he took the trouble to learn Lithuanian, which then led to the creation of a website in the languages spoken by the largest groups of immigrants in Norfolk, and which includes basic information on topics such as obtaining a National Insurance Number and opening a bank account. Finally, with the confidence gained from undertaking these acts, he taught the new residents of his city how to build social capital, how to trust each other and how to create community.

In the second scene we move near to Lampeter, a small, sleepy Welsh town, whose residents decided to take matters into their own hands and, rather than wait for the global energy crisis to strike, transform into a Transition Town – one which prepares for life in a world without oil. The process is just beginning in Lampeter and people are simply interested in talking, listening, and thinking. This is the first principle of Transition Towns. The Transition Town Initiative is a social movement and one of its final principles concerns entailing the support and action of politicians.

In the third scene we are still in the UK. This time, in East Manchester. It is one of many areas managed by government programs for the regeneration of neglected urban areas. One of these programs, of which Neil Smith is so critical, describes the emergence of so-called 'cities of retaliation', in which the poor are increasingly pushed out of attractive sites and marginalised.[40] East Manchester's regeneration program was intended by its authors and executors to regenerate not only the space (preparing it for the more privileged citizens), but also its people. New East Manchester is both an urban and social program. Within these generally outlined circumstances, I would like to draw attention to one situation in particular that occurs within the ongoing regeneration of Manchester. To the house where one representative of the local margins of society lives – a man who does not work and sometimes beats someone (usually his wife), who sometimes steals and drinks far too much – comes a policeman. The program EMBRACE (East Manchester Burglary, Robbery and Auto Crime Project) visits our delinquent up to four times a week, and presents him with job offers, additional education and reminders that he has an eye on him.[41] Carrot and stick. Take your pick: you can still be a full citizen – we can help you – but you have to want and agree to our terms and conditions.

Is the Plug-in Citizen I'm looking for hiding in one of these three scenes? No. But here, and in the previous chapters, are the clues that lead us to it. These clues are local involvement (a banal clue, but no less important than the others), administration and violence. Generally speaking, a Plug-in Citizen is someone who is a user and 'ruler' of the city. Their relationship with the city is one of influence, through free access to existing power structures – the economy, culture, all social structures. Of course, there is no possibility here of a classic, representative democracy – quite the opposite – because the possession of the city by Plug-in Citizens constitutes management under a modified direct democracy. One could call it 'intelligent direct democracy'. This concept presupposes complete freedom of access to the structures of the city for both residents of the city and for temporary residents, even tourists.

It also implies the opportunity to become part of the urban community, even if the (Plug-in) citizen is not physically present in the city. Access to the structures of the city is completely free, but it is mutually influenced by both these structures and the subjects accessing them. Every relationship is individually negotiated.

Let's get back to the beginning. The idea of the City was lost with the ideas of Empire and Church because of its singularity, its particularity. But it is precisely this feature of the City that may become an opportunity today to oppose a unified model of the global world. Cities could take up this challenge but must transgress themselves while at the same time remaining themselves. City must become a universal model while at the same time facilitating very special and unique permutations. Universality and openness are fundamental features of a Plug-in Citizen. If political, social and economic rights, which can benefit people today, are a special kind of privilege which pushes into the background all those who cannot obtain citizenship, and if deprivation creates multitudes of *homo sacer* – people who lose their basic human rights (as argued by Hannah Arendt and supported by Giorgio Agamben, they do not exist beyond the rights of the citizen), then my answer, the Plug-in Citizen, involves a system in which inclusion is a simple act of will. A Plug-in Citizen of any city is someone who wants to be a part of it. I will discuss the philosophical basis for this solution in the following chapters, but for now I want to focus on the kind of technology involved in the operation of the Plug-in Citizen.

The universal possibility of 'plugging in' to the system must be based on the existence of an 'inviting' external interface, which will support this, and on the existence of internal algorithms to which the functioning of the Citizen's Plug-in system will be adjusted. A system for the City of Plug-in Citizens that can effectively transform the city into a political community must be controllable. But how to manage a structure in which management can oversee every person in the world, if only they wanted to become a part of this structure? And how can we think of something that at first glance sounds like an absolute utopia? Or even – let's not be afraid of strong words – crap? Universality of plugging does not yet mean identical participation in the internal algorithms. Plugging in is the beginning of a process; the process of matching the specific, unique otherness of the Plug-in Citizen to the uniqueness of the City – to other Plug-in Citizens. Participation in the structures of the city is in fact different in each case. The citizen enters into an intimate relationship with the structure of the City and through the uniqueness of this relationship – resulting from mutual matches – becomes rooted. The expression of desire to become a Plug-in Citizen is associated with the declaration of local involvement. This involvement, however, is but the first, basic step. To be able to become truly involved with the (at this stage) alien system, the system needs to take control of the 'freshly stripped', plugged in citizen. The City must have an algorithm for administering its most precious resources – and therefore its citizens. If the basis of social relations in the City becomes the Me-You relationship, instead of Me-System-You, then government must manage precisely this relationship – because the system, obviously, is always implicitly in the background. There is thus always the need for an interface that allows a Me-You relationship. However, there remains the question of the ideological, semantic content of such an interface. To what extent is it a 'pollutant' of the relationship and to what extent does it become a third party in the intimate Me-You relationship? Administration must be 'empty' – administration as a pure technology, existing only in the relationship between partners. The system would therefore exist only in the relationship between Me and You. Without Me and You there could be no 'system'.

Here comes the third clue – violence. There is only one task in the algorithm for administering the City: the relation of different forces and the prevention of any blockages in these relationships. The power of a man turns and opens a tap; the same force chops wood and cuts heads. City, to exist, must have corporeal strength – the strength of administration and the enforcement of voluntary reporting. Another paradox? Can forced relationships be voluntary? A City of Plug-in Citizens is a community conscious of its responsibilities. It is a community whose mission is – as in Aristotle's Polis – to cultivate virtue. Each of the citizens gives the City what they can and receives what they need in return. The internal control algorithms of the City administration maintain the integrity of these relationships. They are based on voluntary self-control and negotiation. Participation in the system is combined with openness and sincerity. A Plug-in Citizen gives as much of themselves as they want to give, and receives an equal amount in return. Power is knowledge – knowledge about the disclosure associated with dealing with power (which is why totalitarian regimes try to know everything about their citizens; the more they know, the easier it is to manipulate them – though it is simpler to just exercise power). In today's world, however, knowledge about us is everywhere and is collected by organisations and institutions over which we have no influence. We cannot stop this process. We are not able to function in the modern world without revealing ourselves. From the information that we leave, specialised software packages are already able to build reliable and nearly complete character profiles. This is one of the key elements of the commonly perceived dilution of power, which I mentioned at the beginning. It is not an illusion – the knowledge about us, which gives power, dissipates. However, since it exists inside the algorithms managing global corporations – selling us books, shoes, food, suggesting films for us – when these algorithms need to have power over us (often with the government as a driving force) there is a sudden accumulation of that dispersed knowledge.

The problem of lustration in post-communist communities, namely the disclosure of informers to the security forces and the communist political police, is a perfect illustration of a situation where knowledge is power. However, this knowledge/power does not belong to citizens, who were harmed by the security services, but to the state institution, politicians and journalists. Controlled leaks, slander and gossip are a great tool for control and manipulation. In a City of Plug-in Citizens, access to the records of security forces would be universal... but only to those to whom they relate and to those who themselves dare to disclose information about themselves. Any institution that falls between a perpetrator and a victim becomes the tormentor, because it usurps the right to represent victims. System, which 'wants' to destroy the Me-You relationship, replaces what is happening between people and replaces any chance of a community built on strong relationships of mutual respect. When an informer to the communist security police ruins someone's life, a drama takes place between people. Thus a drama of forgiveness or reparation should also play out between these individuals. What is the use, then, in looking for an institution which is transcendent (external) to these individuals? The same principle should apply to any crime – it is not for an institution to act like God on behalf of the victim to punish the criminal, but an institution should be able to facilitate, or even force, the restoration of balance. How this happens, and on what basis, must remain *within* the Me-You relationship. Guaranteeing symmetric access to knowledge and forcing equal participation in the system is the sole purpose of the internal algorithms of the City. Knowledge/power that citizens have about the City and themselves creates Polis. It creates a self-conscious community, responsible for itself, giving protection and liberation.

III.

Intimate

The Inhabitant of a Peripheral City

III.I

When using the term 'peripheral city', I am aware of the intangibility and even non-existence of a sufficiently precise definition of such a city. Writing about the 'inhabitant of a peripheral city', I know that the problem becomes even greater. Although we can initially agree on a division into central states (which are the main beneficiaries of globalisation), semi-peripheral states (with participation in globalisation, but which primarily exist as markets and sources of cheap labor) and peripheral states (on the margins of globalisation), the adoption of a similar classification in relation to cities is very risky. First of all, because no such division would account for national borders and, additionally, because the internal structures of cities are often comprised of both central (in the sense of active participation in globalisation processes) and semi or fully peripheral elements. So I think that, while recognising the classification of global cities by GaWC as a starting point, it would be more effective for the initial adoption of the division only with global and peripheral cities, considering the blurred and controversial nature of this distinction.[42] In this chapter I would like to focus primarily on the inhabitant of the city, and not on the city itself. The city is the backdrop, simply an environment in which a person lives, but whether they feel they are the inhabitant of a peripheral city does not solely depend on the type of city in which they have come to stay. Residents of deprived boroughs in New York or London will be very much more – in the existential sense – city dwellers than those living in the rich districts of Warsaw, Calcutta and São Paulo. So the key is not so much a recognition of the city as global or peripheral, as classified by GaWC. What matters is how the full potential of the city can be used to put oneself into an existentially global or peripheral position.

A resident of a peripheral city is then more of an existentially and socially conditioned figure than a geographically defined one. However, there are objective conditions that allow people to feel like the residents of a metropolitan centre; social security, a large and secure labour market, access to services, easy access to entertainment and, finally, ease of communication with the world (both virtual – for example, through urban Wi-Fi networks – and physical – via railways, sea and airports). There is also the very important and often ignored factor of language. The existential situation of an English-speaking person is quite different to that of someone whose native language is Estonian, Lithuanian or Swahili. Language, as I will try to prove later in this book, is a crucial element that affects the functioning of communities in space. But how to describe the existential situation of this city dweller? The inhabitant of a peripheral city has first of all an acute sense of lack in their existence. A lack of influence and a lack of meaning. They experience with a special horror the 'life on the grind' as defined by Bauman. Clearly, this description will affect almost equally big cities, towns or villages lost in the world. To attempt distinctions, however, is to ignore the fact that what is more important is our overcoming of the centre-periphery dichotomy altogether, because the existential situation of the city matters more than its classification in these terms.

If, broadly speaking, a global city resident (as an existential figure) is a person holding a share of power – someone with a sense of meaning and potential impact on their fate and the fate of the world – then a resident of a peripheral city is the opposite. Someone who is outside the mainstream of global-local conflict, and even beyond the logic of the 'glocal'. Though it may sound perhaps like a kind of existential desuburbanisation it is in reality, however, just the opposite.

I have always defined City, as a political idea, as the idea of a community managing itself. A political community of inhabitants who govern their own city, the members of which group seek legitimacy of power within the community, as citizens, and not outside it. For if an inhabitant of the city is a member of the global elite then they cannot be a 'proper' citizen – there will always be a conflict of interest which prevents their full, local participation. However, if they are a local inhabitant of the city but have no political influence within it then, again, they cannot be a 'proper' citizen of the city. Neither residents of global cities, who are part of the transcendent, nor residents of peripheral cities, shackled to their physical locations, can create and affect their City as a political idea, as local, existential figures. For this reason, an escape beyond the centre-periphery dichotomy lies not outside the city but inside it. Today, both the centre and the periphery are being desuburbanised in the same way – the City is an escape and an overcoming.

But back to the peripheral city dweller. The characteristics of such a city are in fact trivial: a peripheral city is on the run, a city whose purpose of existence and operation is to 'catch up' with global cities, catch up with the Centre. In this kind of city the only acceptable activity – socially or politically – or indeed way of life is complicit in this 'catching up'. As the only measure of development for the city today is the state's budget, the amount of investment from and the quantity and quality of relationships with transnational structures (such whims as those involving a parametric definition of quality of life in the city can only be afforded by the 'central' cities, those which are stable and no longer have to 'chase'), then the only acceptable activity for a city dweller is to grow material prosperity. Here we touch on the basic mechanism for the production of peripheral people: a radical narrowing of the range of acceptable and possible activities, which offer the potential for survival, leads to the production of diminished people; slaves who are unable to see their slavery. Compared to them, the rich kids living a stone's throw from the cities of the Centre actually live on another planet.

The inhabitant of a peripheral city may decide to choose – unless this choice is made for them – passivity. This passivity, however, a refusal to participate in the chase, condemns them for being outside the scope of what is socially and politically acceptable for residents. One former mayor of Riga proclaimed that the poor should be pushed out of the city to make way for the rich, meaning not so much the 'really' poor as those who accepted their poverty, who had reconciled themselves to it. In the peripheral city, a city that is chasing the Centre, the logic of war prevails: those who are not with us are traitors and should be excluded from our community. The same logic applies to the pushing of the poor from rich neighbourhoods undergoing gentrification in the West; the same logic situates social housing on the outskirts of the metropolis, in the worst neighbourhoods, the least attractive areas clearly separated from the 'healthy urban fabric'. I have written about the 'war' style of management in the context of Singapore but a similar state of heightened alert also exists in central cities – in the context of the 'war on terror'.

A look at the spaces of everyday life actually in a state of war, or at its edge, brings us to very interesting conclusions. Rachel Kallus, for example, describes life in Gilo, a fortified Jewish settlement on the outskirts of Jerusalem.[43] This district is under attack from a nearby district of the Palestinian territories, which forced Gilo to fortify not only the district's central buildings and perimeter but also every house, every window. She rightly notes that private space is thus appropriated by the national (state) rhetoric, ceasing to be an intimate refuge and instead becoming a bridgehead and manifestation of the state. I will elaborate on the disappearance of private space in urban areas, through the privatisation of public spaces, later.

In the previous chapter I mentioned a police initiative that forces socially marginalised people in Manchester towards a social 'conversion', but what about those who do not want to convert, or cannot? Where is the limit of acceptance for antisocial behavior? Certainly in urban centres it is much farther than in the urban periphery, but the logic of expulsion still remains. Can we move beyond this logic? Can we think of a model in which everyone – absolutely everyone – will be involved? Peripheral urban dwellers want to be involved with, and try to stay in, the 'chasing' group. They do not have a choice, however – to remain out of the group could mean death, or at best vegetation. The peripheral city, which thus 'chases the Centre', has one more characteristic feature that distinguishes it from the people of the Centre and the peripheral urban dwellers who do not wish to chase – in addition to the processes of globalisation that are at work and which concerns the breaking of social bonds. Peripheral cities disintegrate pre-urban communities and because, as I mentioned, they are characterised by a narrowing of acceptable social and political choices in life, they do not leave any room for the formation of new, purely urban, durable social ties.

It is interesting that a city which has only recently joined the race – and which has a traditionally tight social fabric, just as in Asian cities – characterises communities with a relatively high potential for social capital. Post-socialist cities have preserved very little of that social capital. It is interesting because, as I have said, the cities of Asia have never been autonomous political entities, and thus the communities of these cities are still closely associated with their 'extra-urban' communities: family, clan, religious. Asian cities do not have this characteristic of European cities: of forced uprooting and the alienation of their inhabitants. This social disintegration can be observed in one of the richest cities in the European Union, Dublin. The prosperity which this city has recently experienced demolished its traditional social relationships, and obsessive consumption leaves no room for the creation of new ones. Despite the fact that Irish society is composed of mainly rural traditions, the power of alienation in Dublin is greater than the strength of the non-urban ties. It should be noted, however, that some parts of Dublin have a migrant population of over 50%.[44] And immigrants, as we know, are a quite specific type of population.

In short, the inhabitant of a peripheral city is working in pursuit of something that they have no chance of catching up with. But there is no other way – the traditional social bonds which would have provided them with a necessary base, stemming from the mere fact of being a part of them, are broken, and the new bonds, even if they are likely to arise, are weak and focused more on participation in the entertainment industry than on support in adversity. An inhabitant of the Centre, by the very fact that they are in the Centre, has a much larger area of possibility in which they can operate. Having origins in the Centre – with minimal effort – guarantees security and the illusion of having an influence on one's life and on the surrounding world. Being an inhabitant of the Periphery and an inhabitant of the Centre are two completely different experiences, existentially and socially. However, there is probably something that unites them – a fear and a dream. The fear of the Centre dweller that they will be pushed out to the Periphery, and the hope of the Periphery dweller that this is possible. However, what unites them mentally, in essence, creates an almost insurmountable barrier. As an old proverb goes – the satisfied won't understand the hungry.

III.II Everyday Life in a Subjective City [45]

The world in which we live is a strange structure, shaped by accessibility and also by the lifestyle, cultural capital or habitus of other human beings. 'Home', as a territory or known and used space, is comprised of disconnected bits of places – like someone's house or flat, part of the street they live in, an airport or train station, and the office they work in a thousand miles away. Modern human beings are still territorial but the period of serflike attachment to land has ended, and probably forever. Today, a growing group of people are defined not by their place of birth but by the place of their choice. Increasingly, we have to deal with changes in these decisions. In such a world, what really defines a person is what is possible for them at each place – and where they choose to move. This is contemporary nomadism. If we could afford a slightly hysterical and radical hypothesis, we could say that homelessness is actually a natural state of being. All of the rituals and ceremonies designed to make a space into a home sooner or later turn out to be worth less than imagined. Of course, a person is a reality of both a physical and physiological nature. They have a body and this body still has a location. But it is the body that is the only true place and – in the most intimate sense possible – a person's real home. A nomad or homeless person is able to maintain possession of their own body and remain detached from the space around them. Others feel only the need to tame and to appropriate a sphere around them.[46] Kevin Lynch began his research on 'mental maps' in the early 1960s. Mental maps are the ideas of space, which allow us to live, that we carry inside our heads. A mental map is thus a map of a 'subjective city'. Lynch, however, was less interested in the fact that each of us receives and 'sees' the city a little differently, and more interested in what is common to all perceptions. The fact that each of us lives in a different city can only create a sense of powerlessness. For the scientist and city planner, however, this observation is in fact worthless. My own position cannot be defined strictly in terms of any specific profession and for me, besides the physical structures composing the city, there is also a subtle and utterly subjective 'flavour' to it. Investigating this further, I asked several people from Katowice, Warsaw, Gdańsk and Wrocław to identify different sites in their cities – the areas in which they live and actually use, and those in which they do not operate and do not know at all. The 'in between' areas remained, but they are not important to me at this time. The results of these studies have shown not only that the subjective city, the city in which we 'really' live, is clearly smaller than the city itself, but have also shown that subjective cities have a discontinuous structure – they are often irregular trimmings, separated from each other. However, the most interesting and most surprising result of these studies was the assertion that the size of each of these discontinuous cities, in which subjects operate, does not differ significantly one from to another. No matter how large the city in which we live, the subjective city – in which we 'really live' – does not usually surpass a territory of a couple of square kilometers.

It is probable that with additional tests about the usage of this space, it would turn out that we are able to explicitly specify the type of attraction and 'wealth' of the city area which absorbs the user to a certain extent and for a specified period of time. We could then try to determine fairly accurately how much such a parameterised urban space can provide for the average citizen. In fact, it is obvious that due to the limitations of the human space in which we actively operate, this would be strictly limited. Studies on the relationship between human activity, space and time date back to the 1960s and are associated primarily with the Department of Geography at the University of Lund (in Sweden), but they did not go far beyond the study of diagrams showing local activity.[47] However, the concept of 'subjective cities' does not concern districts or parts but a city as a whole. Now, back to Lynch and its structure. Based on his research, he concluded that people will recognise some of the characteristic spaces of the city and be aware of certain places, points and lines that compose these spaces. Lynch singled out these five elements: paths and roads, characteristic structures, nodes (or focal points), districts and edges.

Together, they create a skeleton structure of space which we carry inside. Although each of us will classify these elements slightly differently, the fact that they are recognisable by most users of the city allows them to communicate with a certain level of generality. These basic elements of the structure are such that the subjective cities are also to some degree similar to each other. One could say that the basic structure of the city is (or should be) common to all. But is it really so? Is there a general structure that each person can understand, know and recognise in a similar manner, and upon which they impose their own preferences, their own hierarchy, their 'taste' of space? Or is it the opposite – that each of us lives in a different universe, in another space and another city, and only the fact that we communicate with each other means that we 'agree' on a basic structure? The fact that certain elements are structural and others are not has resulted from the ease with which we can label and identify them. Is this not the same thing? And even if not, does it have any meaning – how the elements of the community's mental map of the city are formed?

The city is a machine which forces us to interact. The city, despite its power to alienate and uproot people from their 'natural' communities, also has the power to create a community from these individuals – even if only a temporary one. The apparent, legible structure of the city will, therefore, ensure that we feel safe and 'cared for'. The problem with today's cities – and not just the giants, the big cities – is that their structure has ceased to be clear and unambiguous. The fall of meta-narratives, the dominant religions or ideologies, has meant that the city does not tell a single spatial story but instead mumbles a lot of different stories. There has been a breakdown of community and a disintegration of space; privatisation has turned a citizen – a member of a political community – into a consumer-individual. But this privatisation did not liberate us. Huge malls and retail parks closely examine the routes by which they are reached by their customers. Public transport routes are led towards the greatest density of population, for both commercial viability and public service. In all these cases, we are treated as individuals – particles that are moving here and there with Brownian motion – simply responding to the application of forces that cause us to move where 'they' want us to go. The breakdown of the overall structure of the city is concurrent with the creation of structures for commercial services. Lynch's five elements have been substantially reduced to three: the supermarket, the high street and the local tourist attraction.

The functional breakdown of the urban structure, however, did not begin yesterday. As communication in the city ceased to move on the legs of its citizens – as carriages and then cars, buses, trams and subways finally developed – the city gradually lost its continuity. Its structure has increasingly become the point. Of course, we can speak of a network of related points but the bonds themselves have, after all, no value. It is not an advantage but rather a problem that in order to get from point A to point B we need to adhere to strict timetables. In fact, our city is composed of subjective pieces of a real, existing city (as well as other towns, villages or environments) that are made into one piece but are, unfortunately, cracked internally. As it stands, it is not likely to become a network in which the availability of individual nodes can be managed in a different way, but instead a hierarchical 'palace of the imagination'. The gaps in this palace, the time spent moving from one 'room' to another, fill one's life – with listening to music, reading books or magazines, giving up dreams, and bowing one's head in thought.

Whether we like it or not cities are, for their citizens, becoming more and more subjective. These personal cities, the citizens' own spaces, are much more important and more pronounced than the structures designed by town planners. Yes, architects are still able to create facilities that will stimulate our imaginations – they are still crazy and extravagant – but they are only elements of the pop-cultural soup in which we all swim. And again, as most of this new architecture breaks with the unambiguous (even minimalist buildings tend to be rich in context), each building is a little different to each one of us. Urban decay is shaped by the existence – and size – of these subjective cities. The division between better and worse districts is no longer because of better and worse residential areas, but instead because of degradation in the urban spaces which are used by different social groups, who often have nothing in common with each other, for different activities. The functioning of gated communities, close-knit office teams and upmarket shopping centres in the city leads to the disintegration of the city into parts, but only the existence of 'subjective cities' causes us to lose contact with all these parts. If each of us lives in our own subjective city – as a real space in which we work and which is clearly smaller than the city as a whole – then problems arise when there is a lack of communication between these subjective cities, and when there is no overlap between them, which eventually lead to the disintegration of the physical city.

From what I have written, it would appear that the disappearance of the structure of cities and the increasing importance of individual taste is not to be stopped. In fact, if the way we move around the city is as individualised as it is (and will increasingly be), and movement takes place 'out of town' (in the sense of 'mental' contact with an urban space), then there is no possibility of the city having retained a structure that is clear and common to all of its inhabitants. Such individualisation of space, combined with the replacement of the citizen with a 'consuming individual', kills the city as Polis – as a political being. If we do not live in the city as a whole but only inside parts of it, then the rebuilding of a sense of community seems only to be possible – at best – at a district level, and even that is doubtful because of the fragmentation of the space composing these 'subjective cities'. This disintegration of the space in which we live our lives is so common that even the catholic conservatives under the banner of Opus Dei, or those associated with the traditionalist movement, focus their activity around the parish staff and not the parish in the traditional sense. This means that it does not matter where you live in the city (and even whether you live in the city at all); instead of going to your nearest church, you go to that special one with which you are 'ideologically' connected – no matter where it is physically located. However, it seems that the decomposition of the City and its subsequent fading is taking place primarily in the minds of its inhabitants. For it is here that a person decides on the space and community with which they will be identified. If the authority exists mainly in the imagination, then the authority of the City, and the City itself, must be primarily an Imagined City. If you want to bring people back to their city roots then, in addition to the transition through physical space in the urban fabric and the corresponding administrative procedures, a transformation of the symbolic space of the city must also take place. Perhaps this change is paramount.

A Fugitive from a Peripheral City   III.III

Let us return to the issue of migration and migrants. In her classic book *Guests and Aliens*, Saskia Sassen describes how the relationship between the State, the City and the Citizen has changed over the last few centuries.[48] She shows how countries have pushed and pulled different groups of people, sometimes trying to attract migrants and sometimes trying to forbid them entry. Sassen writes about periodical emigration, the great migratory movements – about everything that has shaped modern Europe. I am primarily interested in the active role of states and cities in relation to migration. However, before saying anything about the mechanisms involved in this process, I would like to focus a while longer on spaces.

Peripheral cities, or peripheral areas, are places from which one flees. If they have no meaning and if they are places of exploitation then they naturally exude a sense of prison. Some believe that one day they will be freed from their prison, while others try to liberate themselves. They escape from the Periphery to the Centre at any cost. What awaits them there? It all depends on how far it is from the Periphery to the Centre, both physically and culturally, and whether anyone in the Centre awaits the fugitive. This last factor seems to me the most important. The concept of the Plug-in Citizen that I introduced earlier also has extra-political dimensions – social, existential and biological. A Plug-in Citizen can be transformed into a Plug-in Human Being. A person who must have the ability to penetrate a foreign culture, often in a foreign language inside a foreign legal system, penetrate the regulations concerning work and residence and, finally, must find for themself new relationships with others, with strangers. That is why the key is the mechanism that will be used to install the fugitive into his new living environment – the aforementioned Plug-in mechanism.

Typically, former immigrants serve this purpose – family, friends and representatives of the same ethnic or religious group. At first glance, this seems to make sense – after all, those who were there before know the point from which a fugitive has come as well as the point to which they have fled. But is this an accurate assumption? Since leaving their homeland the peripheral areas will have changed, so the characteristics of the new fugitive may be very different from those of an earlier migration (the misunderstanding by the old Polish-Americans of contemporary Poland and the Polish is significant here) and the knowledge of the Centre possessed by the former immigrants may indeed be questionable. Ethnic neighbourhoods in the big cities of Western Europe and the United States are an example of the fact that a fugitive from remote areas, who is invited to the Centre by 'their' folk, falls into a kind of honey trap – an unstable compromise between two separate realities – which seeks to preserve and conserve a mythical picture of the 'ideal community', which is in reality a projection of the cultural and social relations of the place from which they have flown confronted with elements of the Centre's own culture. Of course, the ethnic communities exist in their own way inside the city-host, but one should ask whether this is best for the city's vision. As noted in previous chapters, the strength of ethnic neighbourhoods is their autonomy and the existence of relations, rights and cultures that are different from the rest of the city. This ensures their competitiveness and attractiveness. But is a sociological perspective sufficient for us? Can the city afford the existence of areas of which there is no knowledge, over which there is no control, and with which there is sometimes no contact?

Cities leading a policy of multiculturalism have maintained an assumption that every community has a right to live according to its own rules and beliefs. Members of these communities are thus only partial residents of the city, and the community is always the go-between; an ethnic, religious or other kind of medium. This ignoring of the individual for the sake of the community, of a group, is puzzling, especially if we remember that the main communitarian charge against liberalism was exactly its ignoring of the community. However, as I have said, neoliberalism is a city regime which combines liberal, conservative and leftist elements – and a common denominator of this pragmatism is the Citizen-Consumer. This means that the City is interested only in plugging its new residents into the economic system. Everything else is outside the City's domain. And because this 'rest' encompasses a lot of people, and just plugging in to an economic system when one does not know the language, law or culture is almost impossible, we find that fugitives from outlying areas acquire self-confidence through belonging to ethnic and religious regimes. This mechanism shows how the reduction of the human being, and of humanity, in the neoliberal regime is dangerous for the city. So the emergence of problems such as terrorism, that grew in the hearts of big cities and which grew in hatred towards them, should not surprise anyone. After all, the Cities left these people, and local ethnic and religious communities, to their own fate.

At the end of the 1990s in Sweden, which is not a particularly extreme neoliberal country, there was a scandal in which it turned out that, among some immigrants, there was a thriving trade in girls who were being sold as 'wives'. It was an obvious effect not so much of the concept of multiculturalism itself, but rather of its connection with the neoliberal concept of the Citizen-Consumer. It is interesting that a scandal in Sweden, despite a call for discussion in the world, has not led to significant change. In 2006, the UK authorities acknowledged that there is no need for specific regulations that would prevent such trafficking of wives, despite the fact that in 2004 they declared that such legislation should be introduced. And yet, trading in wives is only one special case which is part of a larger whole – the assumption of ethnic and religious control by largely autonomous communities over the fugitives from outlying areas. The City exists mainly in the imagination, and therefore as a political community it may be that there exist different systems for the regulation of human relations. The strength of the City has always been plucking people from pre-urban networks. So could it be that in a situation in which the mechanism for 'adaption to life in the City' necessitates engagement with a community (clan, ethnic or religious), there is an obvious and fundamental effect that denies urbanity?

This, what I have written above, should not in any way be considered a call for the liquidation of communities and ethnic neighbourhoods in modern cities. As I wrote in the early chapters, ethnic neighbourhoods have a unique value for the city as a whole. However, it is disturbing to stop the *spirit of urbanity* from crossing the borders between isolated urban enclaves. And nevertheless, there is the need to say openly that the concept of multiculturalism is definitely obsolete. The Left would rather not say that out loud but the Right – from moderate to radical – stand with their heads held proudly and carry banners reading 'Let them return whence they came', 'Europe for Europeans' and similarly ill-informed slogans. Yes, multiculturalism is finished, and it's best not to stand in its defense. However, xenophobia is not only morally repugnant, it is simply stupid. Stupid because ineffective, inefficient and simply anti-urban. As I have written – City is an interaction. The infamous riots in France, which today are the main ammunition of the right-wing extremists, have shown that pushing people to the ghetto and proliferating racism simply must cause an explosion. Multiculturalism was a mistake, not because different people cannot live side-by-side – to the contrary, they can and should. Multiculturalism was a mistake because it was based on fear and on weakness. Multiculturalism means cold tolerance. This is a denial of the City. But fear – fear of the Other – is not restricted to either the 'locals' or the 'migrants'. Both of them are afraid, and both approach each other with suspicion and prefer to keep each other at a distance. Fear and contempt always lead to tragedy. The New Polis, a City of Plug-in Citizens, manages the implementation process and this 'adaption to life in the City'. It does not leave this process to anyone else, to any particular community.

A City of Plug-in Citizens is therefore radically different from a multicultural city. It is still a multicultural city but radically *transcultural*. It is, in a way, the simplest city; modeled on biological excess and the free intermingling, or 'cross-breeding', of genes, ideas, goods and cultures. A City of Plug-in Citizens requires openness and courage. This is not a city in which 'visitors' have to accept the rule of the 'locals', it is a city in which one party and another learn from and change each other. You may say that we have nothing to learn from people who sell their teenage daughters to old lechers. That we have nothing to learn from those who murder their slightly older daughters for meeting with young men. And you would be right! Because being together is not a fundamental right but the duty of every inhabitant of the City. Tolerance was the weakness of multiculturalism; it was laziness and stupidity. Tolerance has its limits. The city that I have in mind, a City of Plug-in Citizens or, as I will later be describing it, an a-androgynous City, is oppressive in its coercive interaction, it is brutal in the pursuit of meeting and mixing, and it is authoritarian in its search of a new, transcultural quality.

If we agree that the key moment which decides the future of a fugitive coming to the City concerns how and by whom they are adopted, how and by use of which *interface* they are plugged in to the City, then the conclusion seems obvious. The City *must* have mechanisms for the assimilation of its new residents. Not only as consumers or workers, but as full human beings. As Persons. This is not about picking the fugitives out of their culture or religion, cutting them off from their roots, their family and friends. That would be a further crime of reduction. The concept of the Plug-in Citizen is about the preservation of contact, relationships and knowledge between each other. The City's knowledge of the Citizens, the Citizens' knowledge of the City, and the Citizens' knowledge of themselves.

III.IV   Freedom and Alienation

"Stadtluft macht frei!" Cities have always (within our frame of the history of European cities) promised freedom, the sundering of the cumbersome ties of clan and family, of the social responsibilities that oblige inhabitants of the countryside. According to the sociologists, what distinguished the rural from the City was just this breakdown of traditional social ties, the diversity of people and accepted models of life and anonymity. At the same time, however, the City is also accountable for (or at least since the Industrial Revolution) corrupt, dangerous places that violate the human conscience and destroy the soul. This double strength of the City – as a force of liberation and as a power of destruction – is basically the same power but with different effects. The City liberates but leaves people lonely. If the City liberates, it does so by breaking them with their present life, by destroying the roots and connections which were forged with people before they came to town. This is a property of the European city. The City, which calls for autonomy, and which calls for recognition of its uniqueness, also calls for a strict distinction between the inhabitants of the City and outsiders. As mentioned above, Chinese cities were never like that. The Chinese city was a specific, stand-alone socio-political model (though for a while in China there were city-states). This destructive power of modern cities is an echo of Polis: the city in a desperate cry for recognition of its political independence. This force is the possessive, jealous Love.

In *His Dark Materials*, Philip Pullman describes the tragedy of children who were cut off from their 'daemons'.[49] In the world of Pullman's trilogy, people are not lone individuals but operate as a human-daemon union. Residents of the City, especially those who have just arrived, clearly resemble children who were violently deprived of some vital parts of their existence. They do not know what happened, do not understand, and are looking for something that could replace the severed daemon. In the end, as it happens, they also die in despair.

The City, therefore, can be dangerous. The freedom that the city imposes on its citizens can often be a curse, especially when they are old, sick and poor. However, if in Pullman's world the severing of a daemon was an act of pure destruction, in the City we are dealing with some kind of initiation rite. Whether the City will have the ability to revive someone who has died symbolically during initiation, whether it will be able to put them back into the community, or whether it will remain only a guillotine that cuts people off from their roots, remains an open question. City, despite its essence of Polis, lost the characteristic of 'community' a long time ago – for many centuries, the city has referred to the agora more as a place of trade than as a symbol of the political self-power of its residents. This mercantile nature of the city was obviously recorded in its genotype from the beginning but it is doubtful that it had to evolve into the form we can observe today. However, the sheer principle of isolation is well worth a detailed analysis. The city is a machine of oppression, a device forcing interactions. Thus, despite liberation from traditional communities and other links, loneliness in the city remains only an illusory possibility. And why illusory? What about all those lonely people, whose corpses decompose for months before anyone visits their houses? What about people who are dying in the underground stations, ignored by thousands of their fellow passing citizens? What about children who are being abused by their parents in the flat next door?

Relationships in cities are side-by-side rather than face-to-face. So relationships do exist, but they are not relations between people – they are between people and the System. This is, in the end, the most serious allegation against the contemporary city (although it has applied historically too): inverting people, so that they face away from each other, and absorbing their attention with something which to themselves and the community is transcendental. Relationships with other people are usually associated with local communities, and often assumed to occur primarily in small towns or villages. If they occur in the city at all, it is usually within the socially integrated neighbourhoods. Side-by-side relationships do not relate only to the big city. They are, as evidenced by Emmanuel Levinas, the basic type of relationship that occurs in the social and political life of Western civilisation. Levinas links this with Plato's establishment of the social ideal in the pursuit of reunification: full and complete union can in fact only be vested in the relationship of individuals to a singular, absolute being. An ideal and universal being. Only such a being can include different, individual and incomplete beings within itself. Face-to-face relationships are, by their very nature, particular and individual, so it would seem that they prevent this unification. Therefore, they are discarded, ignored. Big institutions are always suspicious of what happens between people. So if the City would be the Platonic model of community, a community clearly different from the natural rural communities, then the dominance of the relation to the System, rather than to each other, is obvious.

The strength of the City means that it allows its residents to escape from the intimate relationships tying them to the community, and also that it does not reinforce the *face-to-face* relationships. However, it seems that the modern city has also stopped its efforts to strengthen *side-by-side* relationships. A postmodern city – but also a communitarian one – offers a possibility of return to small communities, and emphasises micronarrative as the only legitimate story after our knocking of the one and only Truth from the pedestal, the only urban Centre.

In turn, the neoliberal city does not care at all about any of the community. A Citizen-Consumer, plugged in to the economic system of the city, is all that the neoliberal city wants. Societies with as long a history of urbanisation as the British have developed a whole set of conventional social behaviors to enable people to live next to each other in an unnatural (if one's sense of the word 'natural' is of any sense here) environment of compact populations. Chinese society, for example, has developed a whole system of rituals for everyday life that allows millions of people to work, pushing and rubbing against one another every day. In contrast to these societies, rural societies, such as the Latvian and Irish societies, have no cultural patterns of living in dense collectives, which is reflected in practices such as the urbanisation of the city of Riga (on which subject there will be more later) and especially in the everyday life of its inhabitants. So while some communities are able to ignore the alienating forces of modern cities, others are helpless against them. But I think that in a situation where the city, as the System, focuses on pulling in and not on the renewed rooting of its inhabitants (even if the city people are rooted in their neighbourhoods, it does not mean that they are rooted in the City), any other kind of system can easily become a threat and, as its cultural defense mechanisms are too weak, then ultimately the city cannot prevent the alienation of its urban population.

The juxtaposition of these two types of relationships – *face-to-face* and *side-by-side* – would involve, above all, the validity of the relationships as such into which the body is forced in a particular socio-spatial reality. It is therefore tempting to consider the *face-to-face* relationship as better and more natural, and the *side-by-side* relationship as culturally imposed, generated and external to human beings. Despite the fact that I succumb to this temptation to a certain extent, I would challenge this paradox. First of all, because each interpersonal relationship is the subject of not only nature but also culture. It seems that the *face-to-face* relationships are not so much more natural, but rather due to their particularity they must not have a ritualised contact apparatus. Instead, this apparatus comes together each time as the interactions of people are worked out. That is why intimate *face-to-face* relationships, despite the fact that they are often deep and are inherently much stronger and more durable than *side-by-side* relationships, seem to be impossible to adopt as the foundation of a larger community – which, of course, the City is. However, it is these relationships that are being built between people and within the community itself, and not between the community and the System, that are the foundation of every community's consciousness of itself and capability of managing itself. We are dealing with a paradox. With the proof that the City as Polis cannot exist above a certain, limited number of inhabitants, and relies on each one of them knowing their fellow citizens. It is another factor motivating us to seek new solutions, rather than try to resuscitate the past.

Alienation is a negative concept, just like 'loneliness' in the Polish language. In English there is a distinction between *loneliness* and *solitude*, where the former has quite a negative meaning while the latter can be rather positive. From *solitude* to *community* is the inscription on the door of a tourist center in Glendalough – the place where St. Kevin lived, one of the most important 'founding fathers' of Ireland. Separation from the world, *freedom* from it, is a kind of personal revolution, which could become the basis (as in the case of St. Kevin) of a new community built on values and relationships contrary to those which have been rejected. As written above, the side-by-side relationship is seemingly easier to achieve in large cities. Attempts to recreate the face-to-face relationships in local communities, neighbourhoods or extra-spatial organisations that exist in cities (fan clubs, sports clubs, schools, universities and other social and political organisations) do not work in the interest of the City as a whole. They create roots and eradicate the loneliness and alienation of people quite apart from, or even against the City. So if the city is to regain control of itself, and if it is to rebuild itself as both a community and a political entity, then it must take responsibility for strengthening the freedom and overcoming the alienation of its inhabitants. It is the city, with all its apparatus of coercion (understood, of course, quite differently to the operation of law enforcement officers or militia), that has to root its people inside itself. It is the city that needs to ensure that children are not tortured for years in the flat next door and that people do not die in the street unnoticed by others, who are hurrying to and from work or shopping. The city is a tool of oppression: it forces us to interact. In public spaces we bump into each other, sit next to each other, and look at each different person – in terms of status, gender, education. The beauty of public spaces is precisely the violence that pulls people from the social network and releases a pure Person. (Of course, this is just an idealistic model – in reality, this release is only partial and ephemeral. But it happens.) Interaction does not exclude freedom, because only a free person may enter into an intimate and real relationship with another person, but the mere possibility of the existence of the relationship is good in itself. So if in the course of these face-to-face relationships the city cannot interfere and should not even try, then it can and should consciously shape their relationship to the System, the side-by-side relationships. Shape them, however, not in such a way as to unite the group around some model, some ideal or some Truth, but only to facilitate these face-to-face relationships, to initiate these relationships. Public space can force people to interact, can even define the way that people interact, but it cannot impose the content of this interaction. As I said, the square is a space in which you can meet friends, prepare a May Day manifestation or a mass. Public space regulates the content of the public events happening within it only minimally – public space simply allows those events to happen.

The essence of the City is an oppression which not only allows but rather forces its residents to enter into relationships with each other. The City, by regulating and managing side-by-side relationships, initiates – but does not affect or regulate the conduct of – face-to-face relationships. The problem of how to regulate these relationships, how to develop them in the Aristotelian spirit of 'education towards virtues', I will address later in this book.

To Live or Survive III.V

The life of man in developed countries has already lost, or so it would seem, its purely biological dimension. Human life is no longer considered in the context of simple survival, but rather in *experiencing*, or in re-living a certain quality of life, happiness, fulfillment, personal development, etc. In the development strategies of cities, the human factor is increasingly emphasised (after all, this is the main assumption of the 'creative class' concept by Richard Florida) instead of factors associated only with the flows of capital and investment.

Of course, we come to Giorgio Agamben who, after Michel Foucault, sees a progressive offensive of biopolitics blurring the Aristotelian distinction between humans as living beings and humans as political entities. Modern human beings, particularly in highly developed countries, lose their subjectivity and 'individuality', become a part of different systems – economic and social, sometimes political – but in each of these systems they are the subject of their actions rather than an entity having any impact on their functioning. The specificity of the privileged caste members of Western societies is therefore a guarantee of survival which enables the re-living of life. That guarantee, however, does not apply to immigrants, let alone members of the investing population centres outside the modern world. Women who are raped in Darfur trigger protests from the West, but the helplessness that Europe has shown in the face of crimes committed during the breakup of Yugoslavia leaves no illusions about the effectiveness of these protests. This manifests itself most fully in the linking of humans to political rights, as identified by Agamben. Despite the fact that the declaration, which provides (or in any case greatly increases the chances of) survival, is a qualification only for the 'citizens of the West' caste. The division between those who have a guarantee of survival and can take care of their spiritual development, the 'fulfillment' of their life (so it can be just about whether the shoes match the outfit), and those who have no guarantee of survival is so fundamental that a hearing in the cities is not taken into account, does not matter. Contrary to more conservative opinions, the 'religion of human rights' is quite an elite sect. There was the scandal of a young Nigerian who was tortured and raped in Poland (we still do not know whether the officially given age, 22 years, was not overstated), whose fate did not stir interest in anyone except for journalists, and then a similar – though less dramatic – case of a legal resident in Poland, a Kenyan woman who was forced into prostitution. These show how elite the club of people is to whom 'human rights' concern. These cases, sadly, are not isolated, and they show how easy it is to sink in the Polish cities, outside the margin of the people 're-living' their lives, and how easy it is to become invisible to one's fellow citizens and institutions. Poland as a country is just becoming rich, and is perhaps not a good example, but similar cases of trafficking in women, who are forced to prostitution, or simply the ignoring – by both neighbours and the city itself – of people who meet misfortune, are actually widespread in countries that we like to consider civilised. These people often manage to survive, but the line that separates them from death is thin and it seems that, over the years, it is becoming thinner.

We may ask whether we should be at all worried by their fate. Probably they deserved all this – through their stupidity, inattention, perhaps laziness, weakness or general ineptitude. Maybe it is the greenhouse atmosphere of the civilised West that makes people lose their natural survival instinct? The 'Crystal Palace' – as Peter Sloterdijk called Europe – is the space in which only moderate temperatures prevail, an area of the artificial and 'imaginary', and which is a utopia. We inhabited this 'crystal palace', which very quickly began to reveal its structural defects and shattered supporting columns. Of course we can convince ourselves that, in comparison with the Brazilian favelas, put together from garbage, or African slums, our palace seems truly magnificent. And it probably is. The only problem is that it is fragile and is not a palace for everyone. However, there still remains the fundamental difference I mentioned a moment ago – between those who merely wish to survive and those who want to experience. (I am not saying that the former do not want to experience their lives, but that they have little chance.) This difference raises the question of whether we should worry about the fate of those who do not have a good experience of their life, living in the Palace, which theoretically gives them every chance to make it happen. This question has contemptuous undertones. Contempt, that we justify by scale – why should we take seriously the middle age crisis of our colleague if, at the same time in Africa, thousands of people are dying of hunger? As I wrote, there is a fundamental difference between people who are trying to 'experience' and those who are fighting to survive. However, contempt and accumulated indifference to 'small' sufferings is a Trojan horse which introduces suffering to our Palace. Suffering, destruction and death. If, however, the archetypal City was a socio-spatial entity with clear boundaries, clearly defining where 'we' were and where the 'outsiders' were, the symbolic destruction of these walls, and the admittance of economically motivated 'outsiders' to cities (i.e. peasants who had become workers), resulted in the loss of this archetypal clarity. Peripheries and slums no longer exist outside the city – they are sometimes literally its heart.

There are districts of London – a city which has been classified as the most global of the global – where unemployment reaches 40% and where earnings posit below the national average for the United Kingdom. Similar areas exist in all major cities of the global world, not to mention the cities of Africa, South America and Asia, where inequality is growing at an alarming rate. The only arguments that could persuade the residents of the Palace out of indifference and complacency are the economic arguments and those relating to safety. On the streets of Riga in 2005 a graffiti appeared, depicting the hanging half-carcass of a pig separated by a wall from a man eating a sausage – a caption read: 'I can't see, I do not wonder'. Not to take a position on vegetarianism, it is worth noting that this tendency to blindness and a lack of self-reflection seems to be universal and natural. It is a defense of our mind from the atrocities of the world. Could we safely go out shopping, laugh in the cinema or eat ice cream if we were thinking about people who are dying at that same moment – often in violent and cruel ways? Could we live a normal life, being aware of rape and violence happening at a time when we are eating our diet breakfast cereal? Of course not. Can we then require of ourselves and of our fellow citizens in Western cities that we abandon our 'frivolous', juvenile existential problems and began to deal with the 'real' problems? I doubt it. Therefore, what we cannot lose is sensitivity and empathy. Sensitivity to every human suffering – and this is perhaps the most serious issue, though it might seem unimportant. Of course we can, and should, make our daily choices in such a way as to not hurt others. The popularity of products with the fair trade stamp shows that we want to be sensitive, we want to be 'good', but scandals such as that involving one company, who employed a Polish woman and forced her to work beyond her strength (which resulted in a miscarriage), show that our good will is not enough. We can be deceived very easily, and our good intentions may harm someone. Once again, though – and people with liberal views on the economy may not like this – we see a need for control and oppression of the institutions.

In urban conditions, the situation is similar. How to behave towards people in need? How to behave towards people begging in the streets? Throw them some small change or – suspecting fraud – walk on by? While meditating over the colour of the shirt that we will wear tomorrow, inside our own flat, should we ignore the strange silence or disturbing screams behind the wall? Not see, not hear, not think – or impose oneself on the others? Spy on them, be interested in every detail of their lives? And even if so – how we are supposed to do it? There is a need for a satisfactory answer to all these questions, but the main thing is to ask. Sensitivity to human suffering, even if it may seem trivial and banal, is the key to everything. By losing our sensitivity to the small things, we lose it all.

The World Is Ours III.VI

In *Wasted Lives*, Zygmunt Bauman shows how the changes in today's world have pushed more and more people from the safe and happy circle of individuals who can afford the *experiencing* of their lives.[50] I have no doubt that, although Bauman's diagnosis is not true in the 'objective' sense – because no one has been designed by nature's System for waste – it is very true in the sense of a created fear. It is not important whether Bauman is right in describing the social reality of today's world, it is important that this existential fear and anxiety about our own existence is real and true. As noted, the level of actual risk depends to a great extent on whether we live in England, Poland or Sudan, but the sense of danger, of fear itself, does not simply depend on our place of residence. Even if we feel that nobody in Western Europe feels the fear of loss of livelihood – it is not, after all, the nineteenth century anymore – the national care system in Western Europe works, nobody gets hurt and nobody in Germany has not the right *not* to go on holiday in the Canary Islands. But the fear of being redundant increases and is real. The feeling of being 'for waste' is not a figment of Bauman's imagination.

In Poland this is still very much a nineteenth century fear; in the UK the fear is postmodern – more sophisticated – but essentially still the same fear. The present system of global capitalism, in my opinion, chews people up without spitting them out because the System lives on people – it needs them first and foremost as consumers but also needs their human capabilities, individuality and creativity. It is hard to say which it needs more, but I think probably the consumers rather than the creators. So we play a more important role when we run around the high street on weekends, with madness in our eyes, than when we try to create something during the week. It is probable that this feeling, that only two days of our week are all we really need, is one of the major reasons for our sense of alienation. Of course, this 'omnivorousness' of today's global capitalism does not concern only these people and relate only to people as consumers. Hundreds of millions of poor people simply do not exist to the System in these terms – but this does not mean, however, that they are 'for waste', but rather that they have not *yet* been developed by the System. This is actually quite funny, since the System thus absorbs everything that is at its periphery, or 'external'. We see alternative movements and avant-garde subcultures become parts of the System, or disappear entirely (but not quite as often), and it is amusing to see the book *No Logo* in Amazon's estore. However, this 'omnivorousness' creates an obvious fear of losing one's individuality, uniqueness and originality. If what I am writing at this moment is also being written by hundreds of other people around the world (in some form or another), and if my thoughts, dreams and personal discoveries are the same as those of hundreds of thousands of other people, then it is scary – because the System continually claims that it needs freshness, needs original people and ideas, newer and more exciting all the time.

The thought that we are not really original, that they will never give us a Nobel Prize, that we will not perform on 'Britain's Got Talent', is an unbearable thought, which we cannot and do not want to accept. The System needs news, it needs something fresh, to hold the interest and excitement of the audience. Nevertheless, not everyone will have their fifteen minutes in the world's spotlight. Globalisation implies that only the global stars count. If in the past we could, perhaps, expect to be spotted in our village, then today the whole world is a village. Beyoncé may be, unfortunately, the one and only, but the number of other potential Beyoncés – copies – is also limited. The global star draws everyone's attention and eclipses the other, local permutations. The same theme, which I described in previous chapters, returns. The System creates a side-by-side community – everybody has to unite in relation only to global stars, ideas and brands.

The system wants our individuality – to a limited extent and only for a moment. In any profession, we see how our creativity is gradually reduced and becomes basically redundant. Interestingly, despite the fact that the modern economy is supposedly based on knowledge and creativity, the range of knowledge and creativity required within it is increasingly narrowed, even down to the colour of the reports you submit. The System of the global economy, by its very nature, becomes stiffer and more conservative over time. It feeds on both our dreams and their realisation, but this only happens for a moment. On the one hand, then, it seems that the system is afraid of real creativity and real innovation, but on the other hand the only thing that could really threaten System is our lack of interest, the moment in which we stop watching our televisions or going to the supermarket. The System forces us into competition and we no longer look forward to meeting others that think like we do, or that we could make friends with, because those others are our competitors, our enemies. The System is set to the individual and, like any real authority, it wants to divide and rule. Groups, communities and organisations are not welcome, because the churches or strong family units (however you define them) are the natural enemies of the System. In parallel to this the System, as an omnivorous creature, creates interfaces into which both churches and families can plug themselves. But it is the System that, through the nature of these interfaces, defines which churches and which families are able to do so.

Being mindfully aware of the overwhelmingly strong social ties that exist, which are confusing to our hearts and minds, I have no doubt that these ties often sustain our consciences and ourselves. The criticism and, even more so, the deconstruction of these bonds, which allow the existence and survival of some societies, has to be handled with a sniper's caution.

The analysis of the Riga Development Plan, in which there was no word on local communities except a sentence about 'protecting the traditional family model', and the whole vision of which is based on the relationship between the individual and the City, should not be a surprise. With a radical attempt, a postsocialist city enthusiastically becomes part of the world System. The System doesn't like it when people unite – under any flag. Even if we agree that the System is our enemy, it is hard to fight directly with it. Nor do we have enough strength, or even any idea how we would fight it and what we would build in its place. I am as far from Žižek's "First let's effect revolutions, and then let's see what will come of it" as can be. The experience of twentieth century revolutions teaches us that revolutions often evolve into a caricature of the system that they wanted to reject. So instead of fighting against it, maybe it is better to fight with it? To become a faithful soldier of the Empire? Faithful and proud? Familiar with the 'barbaric' periphery, and the knowledge of how very bad a place it is to live for its inhabitants?

The fear of rejection, which the System creates in us, is a regular tool of discipline and is used by empires to increase the loyalty and productivity of their subjects. The Empire has need of soldiers and workers. Need of consumers. To exist, we cannot refuse. When, however, some of our companions are condemned to go to waste, this awakens in us the fear that the same could happen to us. And, of course, it may happen. Exclusion is real and the fact that exclusion always concerns a minority does not in any way improve our situation, unless we have any guarantee that we ourselves won't find ourselves in a minority. If, in the nineteenth century, workers were able to unite in trade unions, if the comrades were able to unite to form a bond that nothing and no one was able to break, so can we play with today's system. We can challenge it, while remaining faithful to it. Let the Empire give us bread and circuses! All of us! We do not want to be afraid – we want to faithfully serve the Empire! The Empire, like any power, exists in the minds of those it governs, when people believe in its power and feel part of it with all their might. We are not for waste. The irony is our strength. The irony and existential schizophrenia. We must serve the System with all our strength; build it, consume, create. But we must at the same time, with all our strength, build ourselves. If we were not so nondescript, empty, banal, if we didn't fear being recognised as waste, then the fear of being wouldn't concern us – the fear of being put on the grindstone would not concern us. It all depends on whether we are an unconscious or fully conscious cog in the machine. This is a fundamental difference.

To Each Their Own Paradise

Neal Stephenson published a book in 1995 called *The Diamond Age*, which still remains a very neat postindustrial utopia.[51] What is interesting about this book – from my point of view – is its vision of the world; divided into lots of communities, constructed according to certain value systems. Stephenson's descriptions and explanations of these different communities are such that his book could almost be seen as a textbook of case analyses. A similar motif occurs fairly often in literature and can be seen, for example, among the titles comprising the *Dune* series by Frank Herbert, in which humanity is (as provoked by a Tyrant) dispersed in the universe.[52] In each of these books the autonomous existence of the community, the 'testing' of different but specific and unique ways of life and functioning, is not only a simple consequence of the postmodern validation of all small communities and micronarratives, but also reflects a pragmatic desire to not put all one's eggs into one basket. We do not know whether the model of civilisation which we have chosen is best and whether it will ensure the survival of humanity, so perhaps it is safer to divide and diversify. If today's globalisation bulldozer is trying to cram all of humanity into the same rut of development then we might ask with concern – what if we are wrong? What if Fukuyama is wrong and the liberal-democratic model is not the best thing that mankind has ever invented? The diversification of models of life at the level of nation-states – which so far have been (and still are to some extent) the best and most effective models of social organisation – is slowly ending. Globalisation is absorbed by primarily social organisms at the level of nation-states.

And what about cities? Cities are – as I described in previous chapters – areas of space that have been colonised by global institutions. The rank and position of modern cities is determined precisely by their degree of 'colonisation' by multinational corporations and institutions. Globalisation is, by its very essence, an urban phenomenon. In such a situation, is it not absurd to look for ways to diversify models of life at the level of urban populations? I am not looking for methods to destroy the System but only to 'hack' it. I believe that looking for traces of diversity in the heart of the 'Gleischaltung machine' seems not only a promising, but rather the only possible way.

There are two reasons why I seek a model of political and social organisation for a better future for mankind in the city. Firstly, as the phenomenon of globalisation is governed from the cities, and it is these cities which primarily benefit from globalisation, we can be sure that cities are the best place to try to 'hack' the System for our own purposes. Secondly, cities are the descendants of Polis and are quite different from the national states that arose on the soil of nationalism and absolutism. Cities, at least genetically, contain this specific element of inherent power upon which one can try to create Polis anew.

But how does the City as a whole differ from any of its constituent parts or fragments? From a neighbourhood or ghetto? In previous chapters I spoke of the postmodern collapse of parts of the modern city – isn't that a good and sufficient model of the diversification of ways of experiencing life, by different people and different groups in society? Are these different fragments not enough to ensure the desired diversity in cities? Moreover, wouldn't an attempt to reconstruct Polis (as in Stephenson's *Diamond Age*) mean a destruction of this diversity? Wouldn't the new Polis be built according to a uniform ideological vision and thus be a denial of the City? When Aristotle was talking about the *different people* who create the city he did not mean people of different cultures, religions or languages! If any community is to exist then there have to be strong and clear ideological grounds because any city, state or power exists, above all, in the imagination. After unsuccessful experiments with multicultural societies, which have in fact accepted the strangeness and separation of cultures and peoples who exist side-by-side in the city, the countries of Western Europe are beginning to look for solutions that will integrate the 'foreigners' into the culture of their dominant society. At first glance, such a solution may seem obvious and sensible – after all, it is the 'guest' who should adapt to the rules of the 'host', as politeness requires. Such thinking, however, leads to an increase in nationalist sentiments (on both sides) and, consequently, to violence and the decay of cities and societies. Rather than multiculturalism, or replays of cultural colonialism, there is another way – a more difficult one, perhaps, but the only real possibility. A transcultural road. Transculturalism raises an obvious objection because it assumes that no culture – neither 'guest' nor 'host' – will remain as the basis for a sense of identity for of any of the groups. Transculturalism also has its limitations. It is not possible to create a global culture that would fit together all the existing local cultures. Such 'global culturalism' would be the obvious opposite of the diversification of which I spoke earlier, and it is obviously inconsistent with the search for the new Polis. Violence and oppression are immanent parts of the City and urbanity. However, there can be good or bad violence.

Baghdad was not a safe place in the spring of 2007. The enormity of the suffering, violence and death had led the – at least partially responsible – Americans to take radical action. Unfortunately, the extensive police-military operations, aimed at clearing the city of guerillas, involved the construction of walls separating Shi'a from Sunni districts. These walls were to stop the violence. They were to lock and imprison it. These walls were a manifestation of the basically naive misconception that the containment of oppression, a kind of 'passive violence', can be a solution to urban problems. Nothing could be more wrong – this belief has not worked in Baghdad, nor in São Paulo, nor Johannesburg. Neither has it worked in Rotterdam or Paris. I am anxiously waiting for it to fail in German cities too. These extreme examples show that the containment of oppression is not enough. The city has to use an active oppression, an active violence, to force people to interact, exchange and, finally, become dependent on each other. The new Polis, just as Aristotle's, must educate its citizens.

The phrase 'To Each Their Own Paradise' describes the city as many cities, as many overlapping models that are each 'testing' a different way of *experiencing* life. Each city must maintain the difficult balance between a flexible openness to change, to 'strangers', and its own unique model of civilisation and culture. I am thinking about the City rather than its parts because a disintegration of the city into autonomous communities, into districts, does not make sense – their autonomy is illusory. Only the City as a whole is strong enough to protect and liberate its inhabitants.

III.VIII　　　　　　　　　　A Plug-in Human Being, A-androgyne.
　　　　　　　　　　　　　People Hooked by Their Shortcomings

The key to overcoming the crisis of the modern world is to overcome the lack of a sense of *experiencing* life that is felt by people. One of the fundamental reasons for this sense of the meaninglessness of existence is loneliness. Alienation and isolation from the world and from life. The individual cannot exist outside a context and the world of liberal consumption pushes the individual outside their contexts, referring only to their needs as a consumer. Challenging consumption seems to be too risky and probably impossible – our world exists because of it. Therefore, rather than negate the system and attempt to go beyond it, I would be more persuaded to 'hack' it for the individual's needs.

Let us start with the concept of 'adherence'. Immigrants 'adhere' to a new place of residence only partially – their memory, culture, family, friends and language will always stay with them. Full integration will never happen because society does not exist as a single, integrated local community. A person, to varying degrees, attaches themselves to different structures (social, economic or spatial, such as the Internet, travel, friends, special interests and ideological faiths or beliefs), which inevitably makes them a network being. A negotiable relationship between the different social structures is the key to describing the concept of the Plug-in Citizen. Imagine that some part of a public space in a British city – maybe part of the town square or a pedestrian passage – is isolated, surrounded by police tape and marked 'Citizens Only'. What kind of reaction might we expect? Curiosity? Indifference? Indignation? I guess it wouldn't be a particularly strong reaction – a general shrugging of shoulders. Perhaps because in the UK people who are not nationals are ignored, or perhaps because the citizens themselves do not really feel that citizenship is connected to their nationality. However, if we imagine such an occurrence in Riga then the reaction would probably be infinitely more violent. In a city where over 250,000 inhabitants (approximately 30% of the total population) are non-nationals of the Republic of Latvia, lack of citizenship excludes them from political life – not only of the country but of the city itself. In neighbouring Estonia, people who are in a similar situation have a right to participate in local elections, while in Latvia they are deprived of this right. These non-citizens are mostly 'Russian-speaking', or the orphans of the Soviet Union rather than ethnic Russians. However, Russia often speaks about this group and in general this is probably the most politically delicate topic in Latvia. Therefore, an art installation indicating that citizenship (or rather a lack thereof) may be an important element of discrimination would be seen as a clear-cut anti-Latvian political provocation. The essence of urban space, in the traditional understanding of City as a Polis, is public space. Intuitively, we believe that public space is a space available to everyone. Historically, however, public space is more closely linked with the concepts of citizen and politics. The Agora archetype is important in both the context of urban space and the – not just physical – public space of communication. Public space is thus nothing but physical space allocated to the political activity of the urban citizens. Therefore, free access to public space is considered one of the main determinants of democracy. The problem is that, save in exceptional circumstances, this space is currently losing its political significance. And it is clear that the commercial is gaining in importance. This shift of power from politics (democracy) in the direction of the economy (free market) is one of the most characteristic effects of modern neoliberal projects. This obviously challenges the sense of the political sphere as such. Nationality makes sense only if the meaning of the political sphere is likely to dominate all the other spheres in which a person lives. If the political sphere loses its meaning then – because nature abhors a vacuum – another dominant force emerges. What kind of force? More about this in a moment. Generally, we see today a kind of mass evasion of politics. I do not mean to discourage people from politicians and political activity, but there is a belief shared by the vast majority that it's all about the market and the economy – that there is only one kind of rational economy. Let us note that such a vision – which greatly reduces the possibility of genuine choice – is a vision that not only denies the sense of politics as such, but moreover challenges the meaning of democracy. In this context it is not surprising to find declarations such as 'The increase in quality of life in a democratic society is founded on the efforts of the individual to take responsibility for their own quality of life', or 'Everyone is responsible for their own welfare in a democratic society', both of which can be seen in the Riga Development Plan.[53] These statements are clearly market-oriented and liberal, but have nothing in common with the model of democratic and civil society that exists in Western Europe. I suspect, moreover, that not only in Latvia but also in the UK such statements, testifying to the confusion of concepts, could be found.

So let's get back to the Citizen. If the citizen was to be a construct which equalised different kinds of people – in terms of education, social status and wealth, race, gender, etc. – then we know today that, firstly, the process of recognition as citizens was and is a process that creates divisions and, secondly, the conception of the citizen was too superficial and the differences which it stubbornly tries to conceal are climbing out. I would risk a hypothesis that the power which excludes the poor, women, sexual or ethnic minorities, etc. overlaps and reinforces the exclusive power of citizenship. This weakness of both the citizen and the political sphere increases the importance of the economic sphere. The experience of the twentieth century has shown that politics is a realm extremely vulnerable to the use and strain of ideology, so in place of a neutral political space – where equal citizens, torn from the authority of groups, churches, organisations, meet and decide together – there is a totalitarian, highly ideological power. In this context, the loss of confidence in politics is understandable. This space was filled with the idea of a free market – as a primary tool of human liberation. The free market has no meaning outside the economic system but still continues to gain socio-political importance. According to its heralds, without a free market there is no democracy. Moreover, democracy is too weak and unreliable to guarantee people freedom; true freedom can only be given by a free market.

Perhaps, then, liberal liberation and the superseding of political status by economic status is real progress? Real liberation – and the only way to enable the various minority groups to enter into larger social narratives? In post-public spaces, commercial space eradicates any differences of gender, race or education. The only thing that matters is the financial potential of the customer. Is it not a form of equality and liberation, of which we all dream? Indeed, the high status of property is something that everyone, as we are promised by our neo-mythologies, may attain through hard work. The contemporary post-public spaces that we know – from supermarkets to shopping centres – are clean, pleasant and comprise the public domain. In which case, should we not behave according to specific rules? After all, there are rules and laws everywhere. There is nothing inherently wrong with these spaces – indeed, trained petit-bourgeois society has many advantages.

Coming from a country where it is not proper to ask a millionaire what he was doing before 1990, and where I could come directly into contact with people whose monthly income exceeds my yearly salary, I would like to declare that – if I had to choose in spite of everything – I would prefer to stick with the imperfect and poor construction of the citizen, which at least theoretically equates my rights with the rights of former KGB collaborators. Only when confronted with a naked, arrogant power – with contempt arising from a bulging wallet – can you fully appreciate the value of the idea which is (was?) 'Citizen'. Because even though this construct is unsuccessful, we know well what the 'pre-citizen' world looked like. In capitalist (and even more so, neoliberal) ideology, the inequality of wallets has always been accepted as a natural fact. We also know that property, though it appears to remove any differences such as nationality, in fact only hides them. Having a proper estate is a result of the combination of all these differences and advantages of birth, gender, race, education, etc. The exchanging of the political world for an economic one – the conversion of public space into commercial – is a gimmick which, under the guise of equality, cumulatively introduces even more inequality. Let me repeat once again: the concept of citizen is artificial, external to the individual human construct, a supposedly neutral interface linking the human being with both the political and social worlds. The essence of this concept is an artificial equalisation of different people. The question arises whether the concept of the citizen is at all necessary – why not stay with the assertion that all people are equal and have equal, even political, rights? The problem is, of course, the natural and universal differences that create inequality. These dichotomies – female-male, rich-poor, heterosexual-homosexual, old-young – are too strong for *humanity* itself to overcome.

The first and biggest difference is, of course, the difference of sex. So can we, by attacking this fundamental difference, say anything to inspire optimism in the broad context of social exclusion? Let us try, and let us use the myth of androgyny as a tool. The myth of androgyny is the myth of a person deprived of negative differences. Of course, understood literally it refers only to their sexual differences – which androgyny abolishes. But androgyny can be understood more broadly, as a total exemption of disparity from life, as a *coincidentia oppositorum*. So that there is not a Gleichschaltung of differences but – and this is very important – the combination of apparent contradictions in the sense of a higher order.

Unfortunately, as interpreted literally, the myth of androgyny does not solve the problems that we have with the Citizen. In a sense, it could be even more dangerous. Faith in *coincidentia oppositorum* would be nothing more than faith in another abstract construct. It may be very attractive in relation to physical urban space, but is only another intellectual play. However, it seems that there is another way – the way of transience, imperfection, incompleteness. With this approach, the androgynous myth – or rather, a-androgynous – could become an interesting alternative to both political liberalism, which developed with the Citizen, and economic neoliberalism, which deified the Consumer. Unlike these abstracts – divorced from our existence in flesh, our individual, neutral, intellectual constructs – a-androgyny is inside all of us. In contrast to systems which seek to make sense of incompleteness with transcendence or the absolute, whether earthly or sacred, a-androgyny seems to be a much more realistic prospect.

Instead of the Catholic belief that the abolition of difference and tension between man and woman lies in their integration through marriage, a-androgyny is a concept which does not only tolerate difference but extends it. Incompleteness and imperfection is a gift representing opportunity and value, not a mistake or evil. But let us leave these questions for a while and return to space again. If the essence of public space was founded on the idea of citizens meeting and communicating with each other, today we know for sure that this concept is quite archaic and may only apply in an emergency. When the political system is only formally democratic, the space gains political weight – a positive example of which can be found in Ukraine and a more negative in Poland. Perhaps the Polish situation is more comfortable than that of countries with a mature democracy like the UK – at least we know who appropriates, and in the name of which values, the public space in our cities. We are again experiencing this process, which we previously escaped by releasing ourselves from the People's Republic: the political sphere has once again become a realm manipulated and appropriated by ideology. This obviously creates a very strong neoliberal temptation. The widening range of options in Poland, the progressive breakdown of the main electoral preferences for Catholic-national (and thus political) projects and conservative-liberal (in fact, a-political) ones, is the result of yielding to this temptation. I am afraid, however, that in Poland – but also in other countries such as Belarus, Latvia and Russia – new, technocratic instruments of oppression have been imposed upon the primitive mechanisms of the 'old' authoritarianisms. The belief that one can escape from the ideologised political sphere, which threatens us with a new authoritarianism, into the market sphere, which would give us freedom, seems to me a very dangerous utopia.

In the space of Polish cities, politics is slowly but surely being pushed out by the economy. Privatisation in Polish cities is an example of this. Spaces that once served the Polish United Workers' Party conferences have either been sold and built upon already or currently face this process. I remember when, at a conference in Lodz in 2010, I spoke about the process of the withdrawal of the city from its obligations, of its escape from the public and handing over of public space to private investors, as a serious threat to the city. I was practically ridiculed by a representative from the municipal authorities of one of the largest cities in Poland. This all, obviously, has a broader context. Cities draw more and more people from the outside: tourists, tentatively needed experts, language teachers, etc. They are not yet citizens but they want – and we feel intuitively that they are entitled – to use the city, and its space. But these people are not connected with the city, even if some of them pay taxes. This makes the city – as a political entity – feel that it does not owe anything to these people. They do not belong to the community. And because there are more and more of them, the municipal authorities are delighted to reject the idea of the urban community. The cycle is closing in – no urban community, no people, and thus no need for public space. The conclusion is obvious, but brutal.

What we see in our cities is not public space – and has long since ceased to function as such. Therefore, it seems that our outcry over its appropriation by various terrible forces no longer makes sense. Spaces that used to be considered 'public' are, in fact, spaces forming a communication infrastructure – for both pedestrian and vehicular transport – or a foreground for commercial functions, or – at best – part of the ventilation system of the city or part of its ecosystem. Some of these areas are, of course, the investment reserve of the city. We have some preservation, in the form of markets in the historic centres of cities, parks and squares, but these are insignificant remnants of the 'good' old times. In this context, we can understand the prohibitions on demonstrations that are issued by the city – the spaces in which demonstrations would be held are not designed for that purpose. Hence, it is easy to justify the prohibition of demonstrations because they could cause material damage. 'Public' space is treated as a space that supports a variety of other, mainly commercial functions. Layered on top of this, of course, is a specific, post-communist and to a great extent totalitarian understanding of democracy – democracy as a choice of power technologies. In modern cities there is no space for citizens. Public spaces no longer exist. They are only spaces for users and consumers. In countries with a pluralistic and tolerant society, this transition occurred relatively painlessly. Until the moment in which some people – who today are referred to as alterglobalists – noted that cities belong much more to corporations than to their residents. Today, the losers want to fight to reclaim public space for urban residents. I look at them with sympathy but without faith. Unfortunately, they do not know that there is no longer a Citizen; therefore there will not be space for it. It is all just illusion and imitation. A heritage park.

Communication between a person and a political system, with the help of the Citizen interface, no longer works. The question is, of course, wider – the neoliberal project challenges the efficiency and importance of the political system as such. The power network has shifted somewhere outside the centres to which we were accustomed. There is a need for a new interface and, maybe, the need to join the system without intermediaries. Maybe it is necessary that we grow inside the guts of the system. That we become the unity of the System. And it is not just a political system – it is rather a system encompassing all spheres of human activity. A semi-totalitarian solution of which both rightist and leftist radicals are afraid. The system can be redesigned as an androgynic whole, built from complementary fragments, but even more so – as something surpassing even androgyny, an 'a-androgynic' community in which different fragments are admired and preserved. Do not fight the system, do not overthrow it, but instead possess and reformat it so that it serves the people rather than itself. I do not advocate dull destruction and negation but instead a 'gentle hacking'. Of course, I'm not exactly discovering America – a similar intuition about the application of the androgenic utopia had already occurred to French socialists in the early nineteenth century, and today Hardt and Negri argue against attacking the Empire from the outside.[54]

The reconstruction of the political system is not the subject of this text, although it is of course its ideological base. The practical question to ask is – can we start a revolution from space? Can city planners, architects, artists – all people of good will – salvage the plot and sow the seeds of revolution in our cities? Of course they can! Androgyny surpasses barriers, combines what is contradictory. Such is also the case with *androgynous space*. It is a trans-sexual, trans-cultural, trans-commercial space. It is a space that unites rather than divides. This space contains in itself poverty and wealth, man and woman, liberalism and conservatism. The sole purpose and only meaning of this space is to soothe, to combine and to integrate.

We must be aware, however, that this understanding of the androgynous myth, this construction of androgynous space, will never be. It will remain the stuff of myth, intellectual frolicking. But what we are talking about is not fun – we are talking about life and the body. The use of the androgynous myth as a tool for the regeneration of urban space seems to be a similar mechanism to that described by Jadwiga Staniszkis in *Power of Globalisation*; a mechanism for resolving conflicts through the binary structure of higher order. So this is another – as Hardt and Negri might have written – escape into transcendence. As such, it resembles a fascist integration of socialism and capitalism into one corporate country rather than an attempt to reach the core of democracy – but this is what we are after, when we speak of the renewal of Polis. What I am writing about is not only pure abstraction. I am trying to describe the processes and refine the ideas that are already circulating around the world. Attempts to build the City as an androgynous space – and even generate androgynous culture – are already taking place.[55] In response to the shredding of space and society that has occurred in postmodern cities there have been attempts to overcome fragmentation and to reintegrate, or to try and look at the city in a fresh way. One of these trials is the concept of a so-called *creative class*, formulated by Richard Florida. I raise it here because in the field of popular science it is the most popular and influential idea regarding the contemporary city. It is hard to find a recently published text on urban development which does not somehow relate to this concept. Without discussing the merits of this concept, one can observe its significant commercial success. Florida, citing the classic study by Jane Jacobs, sees the city as a powerful system of information exchange.[56] He says that in today's world and today's economy the key role is played by the element of creativity. The term *creative economy* already entered mainstream economic discourse a long time ago. As such, the conclusion is simple – it is not the incentives offered to investors, such as tax credits or special preferences, that determine the economic success of cities or regions. The key factor has begun to be – and, according to Florida, will remain – the presence of the creative class in cities, which consists of all those who create anything or simply make creative fertiliser. Therefore, for Florida, the important thing is the 'blend' of different people and different groups, which sets the cultural 'boiling point' in the social structure and in people's minds.

Florida links economic success and development closely with the sphere of culture. He argues that success is being achieved by cities and regions that meet the requirements of the 'three Ts' – places where there is Talent, Technology and Tolerance. In the context of androgynous space, tolerance is the most important element. Florida, for example, has noted a remarkable relationship – which has led to strong criticisms from the right-wing circles – showing that a map of the United States which indicates the places where large, compact groups of homosexuals live coincides almost perfectly with a map of the most developed regions in the United States in terms of new technologies. Obviously, it is not true that there is a direct relationship between these two phenomena. The interplay is more subtle than that, but it is fundamental. Florida proves that tolerance of homosexuals is a kind of threshold point for tolerance as such. If society is tolerant and accepts homosexuals then it is tolerant of almost all – permissible by law, of course – human behaviours and preferences. And if so, people who are creative, and thus by definition tend to be different from the majority, will feel good in such places and will want to live there. As a result, such places attract the rudiments of a creative class.

The project of which I speak – the transformation of public space into an androgynous space and the replacement of the citizen with the Androgyne – is a project that tries to give structure to what is described as tolerance. Today, this project is truly revolutionary. It seems, however, that Richard Florida's concept is another neoliberal attempt to resolve the contradictions of the postmodern city. In fact, the purpose of the concept of a creative class is to increase the economic efficiency of the city. Tolerance and the promotion of districts inhabited by homosexuals are in practice often combined with the removal of the poor and non-creative from these districts. This mechanism demystifies the ideological foundation of this concept – again, it is the infamous neoliberalism, annihilating ideological contradictions through a structure of higher order; namely, the thickness of your wallet. Therefore, it is worth adopting the concept of Florida – the most intellectually innovative concept which the Empire proposes – only as a starting point, and then extending it into a-androgynous space.

The citizen is a concept which (in theory) creates a neutral interface between the individual and the political system. We are dealing with an instrument external to the human being, through which it becomes a part of the System. This dual agency is the weakest feature of this concept and today we can already see that it is doubly incompatible. The consumer is a similar concept, but smarter. In proposing the inclusion of an individual to the System through their 'wallet potential', it reduces a person to one of their properties and avoids creating external entities altogether. In the city, the Citizen concept corresponds to public space and the concept of the consumer to quasi-public, regulated commercial space. The concept of a-androgyny that I propose emerges from completely different assumptions. The a-androgyne is a concept that sees man as a porous being – whose relationship with the System is interpenetrated, concave-convex. An a-androgynic person is defined by what they 'have' and by what they 'don't have', and the 'hooking' of a person into the system is made possible primarily through the 'pores' in them – by their failures and shortcomings. The a-androgyne is also the uniqueness of each individual. Quite unlike the concept of Citizen, in which everybody is equal and 'identical' (in terms of their political importance), a-androgynes are equal in their imperfections and in their deficiencies.

What shape could urban space take in correspondence with this concept? How much better could this a-androgynous City be as a place to live in comparison with neoliberal, post-citizen and consumerist cities? What does all this have to do with the resurrection of Polis? Let us start with the latter. As Pierre Manent writes in the already quoted fragment: "[City] is the idea of a public space in which people live together, consider and decide together about everything that relates to their common interests. This was, therefore, the idea of possession by a human community of the conditions of their own existence. This was quite naturally, therefore, also a political idea", and "Cities [...] are 'ideologically weak'; they are something 'individual' between these two universalisms: the idea of empire and the idea of the mission of the Church." The weakness of the city as Polis, or the city as a political community, is even more evident today than in the past few hundred years. As I mentioned at the beginning, the situation of Riga – where over 30% of its permanent residents are not citizens of the city – is not so very special after all. As noted elsewhere, the modern city is increasingly 'occupied' by modern nomads (experts, language teachers, migrant workers, etc.), as well as tourists, and so the percentage of citizens in the city's population is drastically reduced. There is a certain paradox because the city as such, and especially the global city, is increasing in economic importance, and thus also political importance.[57] In Latvia, a seat on the city council of Riga is much more attractive to politicians than one in parliament. The rank of the city has, therefore, an 'external' meaning but it does not have – or in any case has little – 'internal' importance for its inhabitants. One can even venture to say that as the city becomes bigger, stronger and more 'significant', the power of the people living within it declines and becomes weaker. Local democracy goes together with the sense of a shared fate in the city (or borough) and its community – the bigger the city, the smaller the possibility of the Citizen's identification with it. Also, the impact of the Citizen on urban policy is smaller. The contemporary city – as Ewa Rewers calls it – is post-polis. A place where one of the main concerns is the 'problem of finding who has the right to the city'.[58] So we see clearly that the weakness of the modern city focuses on the weaknesses of the City as Polis, as a democratic political community of local authority. This progressive weakening of the city's residents as members of its political system is, of course, being replaced (compensated?) by a fusion of the residents and users of the city within its economic bloodstream. The triumph of neoliberalism, the triumph of the consumer city among modern cities, is obvious. But it is hard to believe that – even if it is a free-market extremist – the city treats its consumer members subjectively. The loss of control experienced by its inhabitants is the cause of degradation in every aspect of the city's existence. The City fragments, spatially and socially, losing its 'urban' properties and functions, and eventually it weakens and fades. Therefore, the reconstruction of the role of the City as Polis is vital.

As demonstrated above, the re-establishment of Polis as a community of people seems to be impossible. The reconstruction of the City as a political force, built by and for its residents and users, requires an ejection of the harmful consumerist model and its replacement with a model adequate for the contemporary world. The a-androgyne is such a model. What, then, is the a-androgynous city? Once again – what could be the space of such a city? The foundation of every city is the sharing and exchanging of everything – tangible goods and ideas. This freedom of exchange is still realised by the consumerist city but – according to neoliberal philosophy – the exchange applies only to material goods. In the a-androgynous model, based on the acceptance of lack and imperfection, the concept of porosity is essential. Man is incomplete, and this incompleteness – the absence of something – makes him a *porous being*. Porosity creates the potential for exchange. The a-androgynous City is porous: space in the city becomes a medium which enables flows to fill holes, and its porous structure is constantly being filled and emptied. But the a-androgynous City is not only a flow – it is structured. The androgyny of the City does not block the flow, but rather the flows interfere with its existing structure slowly and to varying degrees. Where the structure is weak it is remodeled by the active flow, and where it is strong the flow has no impact on the structure. It has a relevance to other tides, as it possesses a kind of fluid dynamics.

Here I would recall an idea that I formulated some time ago about the density of space. I considered 'dense space' as a spatial artifact, which is very limited and weak in its interactions with the environment, and 'thin space' as a building, or any other object, that is tightly integrated with its environment – a facility with fuzzy boundaries. With this in mind, I formulated a new (in a sense) definition of the monumental: the contemporary monumental is a dense area, characterised by objects of worship, government buildings and most public buildings. The idea of fuzzy architecture treats a building as an organic part of the 'democratic' city – democratic in the sense that it is an inclusive space, a city where its inhabitants all feel 'at home', without distinctions based on age, religion, sexual orientation or nationality. The buildings, which I defined as buildings with a densified space, can be in fact regarded as monumental, inhuman, 'exclusive structures'.[59] An a-androgynous City is a city built of elements with varying degrees of *spatial density*. It is not a homogeneous space; it is rather similar to the space of a *city-collage*, as praised by postmodernists. Freedom, the free flow of information and goods, turns the a-androgynous City into one great communication machine. This mutual attachment and craving for contact and exchange constitutes an a-androgynous City. The space of such a city enforces the interaction of its different parts. It is obvious that such postmodern city phenomena as closed housing estates, closed office complexes (tower blocks) or shopping centres with limited availability won't have a right to exist in the a-androgynous City. Anything that blocks, in either a physical or 'mechanical' way, the connectivity of the urban space has no raison d'étre.

This does not mean that the availability of any place in the city must be identical. On the contrary, one might venture to say that the dedication of some spaces – spiritually, ethnically or ideologically defined – would be enriching for the city as a whole. Provided, of course, that – according to certain rules – there would be a flow of information, goods and services between these specific spaces and the rest of the city.[60] Perhaps the whole urban space should consist of 'negotiated access' or a 'negotiated tide'. The a-androgynous City does not destroy differences – it protects and accepts them, provided that the differences themselves are 'thirsty for each other'. But where is the political dimension of this city? The a-androgynous City may become a political community, may become a new Polis, but only in the case of full and free participation by all – and without exception – users of the city in its social, cultural, economic, political and other aspects. While the concept I present here may seem esoteric, I believe it is not. In the next part of this book I will try to present more specific institutional arrangements, which could invoke the a-androgynous City to life and that would guarantee the efficient functioning of the City in which the Plug-in Citizens would wield the political power. However, fragments of such mechanisms already exist or are being tested. For the time being they are associated primarily with the concepts of the *e-city* and, particularly, *e-governance*. An e-city is not only a city of administrative centres to which citizens have access via the Internet, but also a complicated concept regarding the processing of and access to all the possible information about the city.[61] From the size of the budget expenditure to the amount of rubbish on street X. An e-city is then a kind of intelligent urban management.

IV.

VISIBLE

The Spatial Structure of Semi-peripheral Cities
A Socio-spatial Disintegration of a Postmodern City

IV.1

One does not need to read Deleuze and Guattari's *Anti-Oedipus* to know that the world is not homogeneous.[62] I think we all know that, but at the same time we are again and again strongly persuaded that there is a United Theory of Everything. That there is a great key somewhere that opens all locks and solves all problems. There is a concept of Deleuze's, however, that seems to be remarkably useful in the analysis of modern cities and regions, and which appears in Saskia Sassen's recent book *Territory, Authority, Rights*.[63] Let us imagine an extremely complex machine, in which there are an infinite number of gear cogs, transmissions and other similar mechanisms. Imagine this machine, inside which there are other, smaller machines. Each of these smaller machines have a sense of their own existence, and each of them can work, based on a different algorithms, different rules. Thinking about the city only within the confines of its outer limits is a mistake and a dangerous simplification. The city is inexorably becoming global and networked. Not because it is fashionable but because it cannot be otherwise. At the same time, the new Polis cannot allow this distinction – the border separating it from the surrounding region, from the environment – to become blurred. The new Polis has to be able to clearly determine what it is and what is beyond it.

Neoliberalism is a global idea. Its followers say that it is the idea of 'what is natural' and can therefore be used anywhere in the world, regardless of social, cultural or political conditions. For this reason, neoliberalism is a kind of new, secular, universal religion – "Here there is no Greek or Jew, circumcised or uncircumcised, barbarian, Scythian, slave or free, but Christ is all, and is in all." (Colossians 3:1.) But does globalisation necessarily have to be only a higher stage of neoliberalism – a kind of turbo-neoliberalism, according to David Harvey? Is the same logic inevitable in every corner of the globe? Is

Bauman really right (as well as Hardt and Negri) that in a globalised world there is no 'exterior'? Sleepy towns that have persisted outside the mainstream of the contemporary world are, of course, still 'inside' the system but they can also – in some sense – refuse to participate in it. Maybe they cannot be 'outside the system', but the system itself is by no means homogeneous. Both its strength and weakness is its heterogeneity. Therefore, a town can remain outside the mainstream and lose, or be marginalised and fully exploit the benefits and opportunities of globalisation.

The idea that towns develop at different speeds is a controversial idea. On the one hand, it is a description of the status quo – there are cities whose development is staggering, there are some that are rising beautifully and there are also those that are rotting. Although at some level it is possible to describe and classify the processes occurring in these towns and cities, every case is in fact clearly different. Moreover, not only are they different but they *must* be different, so that their differences do not settle into a hierarchical order but instead become an opportunity, and basis, for development. What is the danger of this non-differentiation? A Finnish man once told me once about their official classification of cities, which he draws up each year as part of his work in the Ministry of Infrastructure. Once, the authorities of a town which took last place in the classification a year earlier sent him a basket of flowers and a letter of thanks. A few years before this the town had hired a company to formulate a strategy for development. This company had thrown all the trendy initiatives – such as sustainable development, clusters, ICT – into the bag and the city tried to put this strategy into effect. It ended up in disaster. Ministerial classification helped the town authorities to understand the error and correct it. Instead of trendy initiatives, they spent their money on local schemes – simple, grass roots solutions. Their success was not spectacular but it happened. In the world of McDonald's, difference is an advantage. Difference within, of course, certain limits. Tame, safe difference.

But cities are more than just the products of regional handicrafts. Cities can only be different from each other in terms of their stage of development, and use these differences to their advantage, when their success is determined not by the size of their budget but by their standard of living. In the end, everything comes down to money – but between the internal regulations of the city and its citizens there should be some kind of 'buffer zone', an area of translation between the two based on a variety of factors and outside the global capitalist world. Imagine a situation in which a house is paid for not only with money, but also with participation in community life. Where rent is not only paid in cash, but also in the care of your neighbour's children or of the old lady over the road. Let us imagine such experimental, anti- or extra-capitalist structures. Imagine such an open, creative world. A world liberated from the terror of GDP. If the opinion that "the city is the first and archetypal medium of interaction, and new communication technologies are simply a development and complement to the city as a place where interactive life happens" is true, then before we start to think about the impact of new technologies on the contemporary city, we should try to understand the existing urban structure first – especially its mediums of communication.[64] New technologies, mobile telephones and the Internet in particular, have certainly brought a revolutionary change to our cities, but any future revolution is rooted in the existing tensions and conflicts.

Some scientists, politicians and futurists (such as Touraine, Toffler and Pawley) see the city as "the place where all the unresolved social problems gather."[65] They see the crisis of modern cities as a "social disintegration, misuse of public space and degeneration of behavior."[66] The riots that took place in France in 2005 seem to prove the truth of those beliefs, but it seems doubtful that one can look for solutions to urban crises in new technologies, with particular emphasis on the Internet. There is an opinion that "the new electronic environment begins to perform functions which up to now were served by public spaces; public space previously used for transport, exchange of gossip, demonstrations, exhibitions, parades and performances has lost its raison d'être."[67] This seems a terrible oversimplification, totally unconvincing – or at least it will until, as Paul Virilio says, you find that you can't have a glass of wine with friends unless you use the Internet. Despite the vision that William Mitchell shows in his famous book *City of Bits*, writing that "this will be a city uprooted to any definite spot on the surface of the Earth", we still exist in a physical reality and the city is not losing but actually gaining in importance.[68]

Modern Riga is an extremely interesting city for at least several reasons. This is a post-socialist and post-Soviet city, a city with the highest percentage of people living in high-rises in Europe, a city where the Latvians are a minority and in which about 30% of the population have no citizenship, and thus no right to participate in the political life of the metropolis. Therefore, it is interesting to see how new communication technologies affect and may affect the future shape, structure, and even existence of this city. Riga bears the traces of the dominance of different nations and different systems – on one side it is a Hanseatic city, whose old town is a popular destination for tourist trips, while on the other side over 60% of the population live in post-Soviet blocks. The structure of the city reveals its history – Swedish, Polish, Russian, German and eventually Latvian governments all left their traces, which are unlikely to comprise a single, coherent story but instead create a multitude of stories. Sometimes these stories simply exist side-by-side, but sometimes they interact violently. A lack of clear structure, which can be an attraction for tourists wishing to get lost in the winding streets of the old town (which is small in Riga, incidentally), creates a strange impression of absurdity when the pavements end without warning. The structure of the population's density is nothing like the classic European model, with a strong centre and exclusive suburbs – randomly scattered post-Soviet blocks are the dominant habitat of the inhabitants of Riga. Despite the fact that approximately 50% of the population is Russian-speaking (the official statistics say this is about 30% nationwide), there is a consensus among the Latvian political class to leave Latvian as the sole official language of the country. This agreement is even recorded in the Latvian constitution. Despite the fact that Riga has historically been a multicultural city (one of its mayors was a Scot), today's approach – depriving non-citizens of the Latvian state of any political influence on the processes affecting urban areas – seems to have a slightly nationalistic flavour. One can add that neighboring Estonia, also in possession of a significant Russian-speaking minority, has given this minority the right to participate in elections at the local level.

The majority of Latvians live in cities. From this point of view, they are an urban nation. However, the Latvian mentality is not municipal – it is rural, reluctant and suspicious of the city and its culture. This anti-municipal attitude is firmly rooted in Latvian culture. Riga, despite its status as capital, was and still is seen in contrast to the 'real' Latvia, and is treated more like a foreign body – an aggressor – that has conquered Latvia than something which is truly and deeply connected with the 'Latvji'.[69] Perhaps such an attitude makes its residents leave town on weekends, go to the countryside – where they feel more 'at home' and 'in place'. For if the Latvians could choose, they would choose the countryside over the city. This aspect of the Latvian mentality is evident and perceived by many as a problem. Latvian architects, for example, believe that Latvians can be 'raised to urbanity', but the way that they want to do this seems quite strange: "We agree that tall buildings are one of the approaches that Latvians, generally having little experience with large cities, can adopt to strengthen the city values of tolerance and civic awareness."[70]

As it is easy to predict, the outcome of such thinking is not particularly 'urban' in the European sense of the word – but skyscrapers and detached houses are the most common types of building in which the Latvians live. This situation should provoke a quite basic question – does it makes sense to force people who prefer the countryside (or small towns) to live in a city? I will return to this issue later. It is time to ask a further question, about the potential impact of new communication technologies in cities like Riga. Official documents such as the Riga Development Plan avoid the issue of nationality. They have adopted a liberal point of view and try hard not to notice that, among the institutions of the city and the individual Citizen-Consumers, there are a whole range of different social organisations, informal structures and relationships. In such circumstances, can any of the processes of integration occur in Riga? Is any kind of spatial or social integration possible in the city? The main problem that hinders this integration is the bilingualism of Riga's residents. The problem does not concern the fact that the Latvians are not able to communicate with the Russians (or more precisely – the Russian-speaking city dwellers), because the vast majority of both communities are bilingual and fluent in both languages. The problem is that these communities simply *do not want* to talk to each other.

There is a very popular social networking website in Latvia, as in many other countries, which can be found at www.draugiem.lv (the Polish website, nasza-klasa.pl is very similar in nature). This website is a Latvian-only service but it has a Russian-language counterpart, www.druzja.lv, which carries directly over to the druzja.ru page. The existence of these two sites shows that the 'public space of the Internet' is a myth. If the Russians may – even accidently – meet with the Latvians in physical, public spaces (squares, streets, parks), then on the Internet such a meeting is simply impossible. Language – and even more so, difference in alphabet – creates an effective barrier not only against understanding, but even against a meeting. Yet it is much easier to find proponents of a particular hobby on the Internet than in a specific space which we might call the public domain. Communities inhabiting virtual space then resemble Victorian gentlemen's clubs far more than urban communities or neighbourhoods. Of course, the Internet is not the main factor responsible for the socio-spatial disintegration of modern cities but, as you can see, it seems doubtful that we can find rescue in virtual space. However, if language is the main obstacle to agreement between the two communities living in Riga, and if this obstacle cannot be concealed by the Internet, then perhaps a solution to this situation would be to adopt a higher structure which 'exceeds' the current systems and existing divisions. Each binary conflict may be overcome by using a higher, overarching structure. Just as Jadwiga Staniszkis was an advocate of 'repressing' post-communist structures through European Union structures, so can we think of the language as a neutral zone of agreement which transcends and eliminates the conflict between Latvians and Russians.

Today's world increasingly resembles a feudal world. Could it be that Berdyaev's intuitions were right? However, this analogy with the Middle Ages is only partial and superficial. The weakening of the Centre, the disintegration of authority and its division into strong and independent centres, is not enough to make this analogy successful. The weakening of the Centre is a fact which seems to be the hallmark of our times – from the natural decay of city centres to the disappearance of their unifying ideas. Postmodern micronarratives have replaced the modern (and earlier) grand narratives. The weakening of the Centre is also a loss of the decision-making centres in cities. A loss not so much of authority itself but of *recognisable* authority, the importance of which is primarily symbolic. Belfast, a city which has experienced an unusually sharp conflict between two communities, is now slowly being reborn. This is best seen in the rebirth of the city centre. Imagine, however, that instead of the formation of one centre there are two, three or more 'centres' – and we can no longer talk about any kind of integration. Under such circumstances, integration is simply not possible. The existence of the Centre is primarily the existence of a readily imaginable structure to the mental map of the city. A city without such structure (comprised of, for example, introverted high-rise estates) is a city without identity, without a symbolic power. If the city is powerless then strength will appear otherwise: a lack of centre gives birth to violence. This is, however, not an 'empty' violence – the kind of oppression I would like to see in the city; a violence forcing interaction, a violence creating and liberating. A lack of centre is precisely a lack of this 'empty oppression' and its replacement with local gangs and violence. Of course, it is not true that any centre or any central authority is the remedy for all problems (I will soon return to a pseudo-Deleuzian model for the city as a conglomerate of different autonomous machines, operating according to specific algorithms). The city simply needs symbolic mechanisms that will create reference points for its residents. I repeat once again – a symbolic central authority, a symbolic centre, help residents to find common points of reference. The lack of such a symbolic centre leads to the unbridled struggle of everyone against everyone else. A lack of centre – at least a symbolic one – provokes violence which is, unfortunately, not symbolic.

IV.II   NEIGHBOURHOOD COMMUNITY IN A SEMI-PERIPHERAL CITY

In *Religion in the Public Sphere,* Jürgen Habermas writes of the 'discrimination' against religiously motivated discourses in the public debates of liberal countries (with the obvious exception of the United States). He tries to weave religious language into the language of public debate, while keeping lit the 'fuse' which bans the use of religious arguments by politicians. To paraphrase him: let us not make 'ordinary' people with a religious orientation 'translate' the language in which they live – that is, religious language – into the language of the secular, because it discriminates them against those of 'secular orientation' and whose language is naturally the 'official' language of the state. Let us leave this obligation of translation, he says, to politicians. Politicians are already becoming a kind of a specialised caste of interpreters of 'popular' language(s) – including religiously motivated language, the language of the secular state and other ideologically neutral states. This view is interesting for several reasons. First, according to the leftist dogma of 'emancipation', we cannot exclude religious people from the political community. This is also because – as Habermas writes – we live in a post-secular society in which religious people have not only managed to avoid diminishing, but in which religious beliefs have ceased to be a carefully and discretely concealed secret. Secondly, Habermas rightly sees in religious discourse an interesting and rich source of 'pre-political' values, concepts and languages, which are in fact embodied in the institutions and political language used in liberal democracies. Therefore, the abandonment of religion would – if we put it this way – deprive the 'cold' liberal project of a significant source of fuel. But here we come to a dangerous point, in my opinion. Habermas recognises as granted 'the modernisation of religious consciousness', which implies consent to religious pluralism, the emergence and development of modern science, the spread of positive law and secular morality.

Moreover, he admits that the liberal state, while ideologically neutral, is in fact a dead project – a clean technology of governance. Here he almost literally echoes the views of various Churches, that democracy without values (implicitly – religious ones) is not democracy. Finally, he tacitly assumes that the secular project is just one of many projects and languages. In fact, he thus rejects – though he tries to defend himself against such a conclusion – the concept of a neutral state as a kind of abstract space in which equal rights can meet different discourses. However, it seems to me that Habermas' intuition is right on many points – neutrality seems to hurt more and more groups of people. Not just the ideologically committed militants under various banners, but ordinary people who do not feel 'at home' in this 'neutral' discourse.

This 'neutrality' has ceased to be regarded as a liberating and equalising language of opportunity and a space for dialogue, and has instead become a space of oppression. I raised a similar argument earlier in relation to the neutrality of the Citizen concept. This 'oppressive neutrality', as a potential zone in which conflicting communities could meet, is in fact disputed by Habermas – and it is difficult to deny him justice. However, some space of encounter and dialogue is vital to us today. Attempts to rebuild this area – on a new basis – seem to be needed dramatically today. However, I doubt whether the modernisation of religious consciousness is an irreversible fact. For casual Christians, ardent creationists and even for Islamic fundamentalists (or fundamentalists of any religion, at that), pluralism is not acceptable, secular morality is absurd and modern science must be judged through the prism of religion, as exemplified by the famous attacks on the theory of evolution. It was Mircea Eliade who wrote: "For religious man, this spatial nonhomogeneity is the experience of an opposition between space that is sacred – the only *real* and *real-ly* existing space – and all the other space, the formless expanse surrounding it."[71] So this 'modernisation of religious consciousness', which would in fact consent to the admission that sacred space is not the only kind of space to really exist, seems to be unacceptable for true believers. So in my opinion, Habermas is wrong to believe that it is widespread. It is not. Moreover, if we recall Popper and his enemies of open society, then religiously motivated people are definitely among them. So admitting religious discourse to the 'vestibule' of the state will open the way to a slow percolation of religion into the realm of the neutral state, which will not by any means prevent feelings of exclusion among religious people (or indeed a return of religious wars) but will certainly provoke an exclusion of people with a secular orientation. The problem, therefore, is either the recreation of a political project in which different groups of people can coexist under equal rights, or the admitting of defeat and agreement on a more or less oppressive authority which will subdue all other discourses.

The problems which Habermas writes about are the real problems we face while considering the structure of neighbourhoods and enclaves within cities. Communities of neighbours – particularly in peripheral or semi-peripheral cities – are based upon strong social ties. These bonds are nothing but social capital. Social capital is in turn very often based on religious convictions, in as much as they have informed moralities which are commonly held among people today. Districts and enclaves, as separated spatial units with bright, clear limits between their social and cultural characteristics, are a kind of relic of pre-urban thinking and cultures. They are a type of village with a closed, almost xenophobic mentality. If social capital can be dangerous, then it happens here. An example of such neighbourhoods may be found in Lower Shankill Road in Belfast. This district is a loyalist island, inhabited by the followers of the two fighting Protestant paramilitary groups (Ulster Defense Association and Ulster Volunteer Force) and surrounded by Catholic neighbourhoods – districts that, in 2007, were inhabited by only three hundred families, while in the 1960s about eighteen thousand people lived there. This district is very close to the city centre so today – as Belfast is experiencing its rebirth – more and more developers and investors are looking at Shankill as a tasty morsel. The problem with this district, however, is its people. People who not only refuse to accept anything Catholic but who, in general, do not accept anything foreign either. It is interesting that although one can hardly speak about theology with them, and their activity is minimally religious, sectarian hatred is at the core of their understanding of the world. This core exists at the level of emotion and perception of the world, not its interpretation. The interpretation of fact is already part of the secular world. Interpretation always leads to criticism, to the questioning of some elements. In the case of Shankill's residents we have a proof that Habermas' hopes are dashed – the way of seeing the world and seeing each other in the world that is shared by these people is a little narrow-minded and uncritical. These 'irrational' (although I would prefer to say – pre-thought) prejudices shape the emotions of these people. The residents of such neighbourhoods are people with a very strong territorial consciousness. This may seem unbelievable for us, but some of them have never visited the city centre which is only a kilometer from their district. In some areas of this kind, motivated by certain prejudices, the inhabitants do not even visit the local centres. The subjective city, about which I wrote earlier, is incredibly small for the residents of Shankill and similar neighbourhoods. This very spatially limited activity and perception of the city confirms the 'nonurban' dimension of such neighbourhoods and enclaves. If we consider the phenomenon of the city – its size, diversity, unpredictability, the density of interactions between human beings and their interactions with the environment – then we will have to consider the socially and spatially integrated areas (in the sense of spaces clearly separated from the rest of the city) as phenomena definitely not, or even anti-urban.

The residents of Shankill Road are not (despite any sympathy for such structures) a criminal, militarised community of totalitarian mentality. These people, and many like them, are a diverse network of relationships, sympathies and antipathies. In the case of Shankill we are dealing with very powerful 'tension' and mistrust between the UDA and UVF supporters. You can also distinguish quite precisely in this community the 'hard core' – the most fanatical and uncompromising people – and those to whom the 'outside' world does not seem totally evil and hostile. The planned regeneration of the district, which was executed in 2007, assumed the preparation of the district and its residents for new investment and new residents. If at this moment only less than a thousand inhabitants live there, whereas the theoretical capacity of the district is eight to ten thousand residents, then conflicts – perhaps even in their most acute form – seem certain. To prevent these conflicts, or to minimise their risk, the current inhabitants proposed that the 'new' inhabitants should be selected on the basis of their association to the neighbourhood. What was meant then was to primarily attract the older residents (and their children) who left the district in the 1960s and 1970s back to their original neighbourhood. There we would have an extended model of sectarianism, where in one place in Belfast we would have managed to gather most of the local Protestant fundamentalists. This model – although interesting – is extremely dangerous and probably impossible to predict. Dangerous because such a large concentration of fundamentalists, built around a strong ideology, would be a machine producing extremism. There would be a ghetto, whose foundation would be hatred for the rest of the city and the conviction of its own uniqueness and purity. Although the idea is dangerous, it contains in itself an interesting aspect which was unexpected by its originators. Even now, the residents of Shankill Road are not homogeneous in their dislike for the rest of the city. Shankill has fragments of fundamentalism but there are people more open to the city and the world. Even a few Poles live in the neighbourhood. The processes which open these people to the world and to nonsectarian values are introduced by schools which thus play a positive role in the district. In addition, the easiest way to dissipate fundamentalism is through money – the present inhabitants of Shankill Road currently live mainly on benefits, but most of the new people who will settle there will buy their new homes or apartments. This fact allows us to suspect that the new residents of Shankill Road are unlikely to be such fanatical loyalists as the present ones. Moreover, if such like-minded residents already naturally draw themselves into a kind of 'circle of fanaticism', then can this way of thinking be extended to new residents? We would then have an onion structure – where each 'layer' of the city would be less fanatical than the previous (remaining, however, sufficiently related to its adjacent layers to coexist peacefully) and the outermost groups could be considered more or less 'neutral' in relation to the rest of the city.

This structure only makes sense, of course, in a situation of distinct, territorially aware, neighbouring communities, living in enclaves with sharp borders. But is such a concentric structure an ideal solution? It seems that this kind of socio-spatial engineering, under these conditions, should work. The only problem is that it is a very static structure. It assumes the immutability of social attitudes and networks, and in addition petrifies the fanaticism – simply burying it under layers of less fanatical fellow citizens. Therefore, it seems reasonable that this structure of 'softened circles', of static segregation, is broken by some kind of social, public or commercial structure (or function). Despite the assumed conservativeness of neighbouring communities, the city inherently provokes revolution and change – therefore, even the enclaves should be exposed to the mild pressure of the 'exterior' and 'urbanity'.

The Lost Myth of the Socialist City? IV.III

At first glance, the existence of even the myth of the socialist city seems very doubtful. For in a world in which real socialism has failed, and in which socialist cities are only an eccentricity – taught as a part of the history of urban planning – how are we to try and talk about the socialist city except as a socialist myth? And perhaps the role of myth, an unrealised utopia, is the most appropriate for this idea? Perhaps the case is neither one nor the other. The socialist, or even just social, city is more than a myth and more than a utopia. The socialist city – as the concept of an inclusive city, a city for all its residents – is alive and surprisingly well. Only from the Polish perspective can a discussion of the socialist city seem bizarre. Elements and ideas of the social city can be found all over the world – from Porto Alegre, the cities of Western Europe, Asia and Africa, to Singapore. Despite the generally dominant neoliberal model, if socialist ideas are still alive and a viable alternative anywhere in the world then they emerge at the level of cities. Of course, the socialist city has always been a much more complicated idea than that which I want to write about here. First of all, a socialist city is a city in which there is no trade of land and no market, so to some extent the land in a socialist city is without value. The consequences are well known and frequently discussed, and I would like to focus instead on other, more intangible and fundamental aspects of these cities.[72]

On 7 June 2006 at Harvard University, Ela Bhatt (an Indian lawyer and economist, founding member of the Self-Employed Women's Association – SEWA) delivered a lecture in which she said: "More than 92% of India's workforce is in the informal economy; they contribute 63% of the country's GDP, 50% of savings and 40% of exports to the national economy. And their numbers are growing all over the world. Yet the infrastructure to support the needs of these workers is minimal or non-existent. Why? Because they have been invisible for too long. Because labour economists and policy makers cannot 'see' them. Because the consensus does not count them. Because they are poor and illiterate. Because they are unorganised. Because ground reality is different from a country's image of itself. Nations want to be modern and industrialised and computerised; we want cities with glass facades and multi-storey car parks. We want to forget that cities are people. We want to forget that our cities are totally dependent on the labour of the poor. Without their silence and their toil, our cities would collapse. Urbanised countries are no different. Without cheap immigrant labour from neighbouring rural economies, survival would be difficult. In the end, a nation is only as rich as its poorest citizen."[73] Earlier, in April 2006 while at the conference on 'World Class Cities and the Urban Informal Economy: Inclusive Planning for the Working Poor', she said: "We are here trying to convince the city planners and developers that by investing in their community and their trade infrastructure, we are investing in a sound economic base for our city. We hope the planners realise that the governance of our cities and their community infrastructures is a big opportunity not only for building an economic base (and not for more flyovers, roads and big convention halls), but also for making democracy work at the city level where it matters the most. Otherwise, what is left for us is hunger and violence."[74] One could not say this any clearer. Aren't the words of Ela Bhatt the words of a socialist? Organisations such as SEWA, StreetNet International and Shack/Slum Dwellers International (and hundreds of others) still continue to express the same desire for equality and justice – for the liberation of the oppressed. The same drive is also present in (at least the declarations and intentions of) Europe; the politics of urban Britain, Germany and Scandinavia. The seeds of socialist, leftist thinking about the city were never entirely removed from the city. Just like the seeds of capitalism.

In the U.S. there are a lot of very interesting urban (or quasi-urban) phenomena. One of them is 'Doughnut City'. 'Doughnut City' is, unsurprisingly, a city with a hole in the middle (a non-American example of this phenomenon is Melbourne). The collapse of city centres is also known in Europe – particularly in Britain, where the inner city is synonymous with poverty, depravity and crime. But it is outside Europe that this fall took on such spectacular proportions. Why? It seems that in the U.S. cities simply do not have the 'hard core' which European cities have, so the loss of the Centre is easier. Interestingly, the rebirth of the Centre in the cities of the UK, and also Australia, is combined with demographic changes. The people who move to the centre are young people, well educated, often without families but with a considerable income. The Centre of the city becomes a centre of entertainment and fun. 'Doughnut City' transforms into – as it was lovingly called in the case of Melbourne – 'Cafe Society'. Of course, without outside intervention the revitalisation of the Centre, or any other district, is almost impossible. Almost, because there are miracles in the form of 'spontaneous' and 'bottom up' revitalisations in urban areas, as Jane Jacobs described in her most famous book *The Death and Life of Great American Cities*. External interventions, however, sometimes bring more harm than good.

The very idea of external intervention in urban districts is a modernist idea. It is also, to some extent, a socialist one, in the sense that the community (which in this case is comprised of city authorities) makes decisions affecting the fate of individuals. So the community takes freedom and responsibility away from individuals – putting it on itself. In this sense, however, the City is by its very nature socialist – there is no space for absolute freedom. Besides, such absolute freedom might only be possible in a hermitage. So if the idea of regeneration is to some extent socialist, then its objectives and methods are decidedly capitalist. What is the purpose of such revitalisation? The objectives can be twofold: either it is to increase land value, and then we usually deal with the processes of gentrification and the pushing of existing communities outside the revitalised areas; or it is about the 'true rehabilitation' of the district, which is primarily to improve the living conditions and quality of living of its community. Such revitalisation, based on the so-called co-participation plan, is quite commonly used in the UK. This 'real' regeneration generally looks for power inside the community and district, not outside it – the 'outside' is only there to help. One cannot help but notice the links between such thinking and the subsidiarity principle, found in Catholic social teachings (and actually written into the Polish constitution). But here we have the same problem as in the first case. A successful revitalisation, particularly in a well-located area, increases property prices and the general cost of living, and thus 'pushes' out at least some of the existing residents. It is hard to call such processes socialist – unless they are socialist in form, capitalist in content.

In previous chapters I have written a lot about the differences and conflicts in the city, immigrants and 'outsiders'. I have said that the transcultural city is oppressive in its coercive interaction. It is brutal in the pursuit of meeting and mixing; authoritarian in its search of a new, transcultural quality. I have pointed to violence as the primary factor in achieving the sustainable development of a city. This is the key to understanding planning – to understanding the city. Spatial planning is, by definition, violence. We are limiting individual freedom, freedom in the disposal of property, in the name of so-called social objectives and the public good. Such statements cause an explosion of aggression in liberals, so it should not be surprising that planning in the U.S. is so bad and that the 'city with a hole' phenomenon is so prevalent there. Nor should it surprise us that revitalisation founded on the liberal concept of the city cannot succeed. While writing about the 'socialist city' and violence, I am not trying to say that a city based on the totalitarian socialist ideology is my ideal. Just that the city – and especially the small American town – is powered by a tremendous pressure forcing it to very meticulous, *aesthetic* solutions. But these are precisely the regulations concerning the appearance and behaviour – and not creation – of pro-social behaviour and the reduction of inequalities that I am trying to talk about. The famous Disney town called Celebration – being, in principle, the essence of what is American – is almost as totalitarian as the Soviet communal houses!

No methods and no words, but only objectives and results decide things. Violence is an inherent component of urbanity, but for what purpose it is used is a matter upon which we will continue to argue. It seems that despite the obvious cultural, religious and ethnic tensions, conflicts and destruction are being caused by class, and not racial differences. Sometimes they are also caused by tensions arising from differences in cultures, where the inability to communicate comes to the fore – as in the case of the Turkish neighbourhoods in Germany. In Riga, we have two communities – Russian and Latvian-speaking – who live in a state of constant mixing and tension and do not establish separate districts. They just lock themselves inside their privacy – destroying any chance of the emergence of local communities. We also have the example of Jerusalem, where the differences concern primarily political rights rather than class differences (class and economic differences are being created there by political and ethno-religious conflict). Also, in the earlier described Belfast the nationalist-religious prejudices intertwined perfectly with the class conflict of the Catholics.

The city is a weave of many trends and ideas. It has descended from both the idea of free trade and (which is essential, in my opinion) the idea of managing each community. The objectives held by the City define its ideological orientation. A city which, 'by principle', is trying to alleviate inequalities is a socialist city, and is different to the city in which differences are obvious and accepted. It is a cliché, but this cliché means everything here. Do we really dream of a city in which the 'invisible' immigrants and poor people work hard for us to enjoy ourselves carelessly? If not, then it means that the myth of the socialist city is far from dead.

IV.IV CITY AS OPPRESSION

I come finally to one of the key ideas in this book: the a-androgynic City (or 'a-a' City, for short) – the new Polis. This is the idea of 'empty violence'. As already discussed, social capital – which still seems to be necessary for the functioning of the city (despite the objections posed to it by Richard Florida, who tries to replace it with 'creative capital') – actually has its dark side: "Particular interests secretly influencing economic activity, compounded with insular neighborhoods, block the mobility of the city; strongly associated groups can inflame social conflicts, and may also divide and disintegrate the community. Social capital can be a primary fuel for destructive and harmful behaviors. Strong communities can be oppressive and conformist."[75] What determines whether social capital strengthens positive or negative forces? And where exactly is the boundary between the two? A generation or two ago, in the villages of northern Finland, young people who were getting married but couldn't afford their own home had the whole community help them to build one. It sounds like a tale from the village of Amish but differs from it in one very important detail. Despite being Christians, Finns did not and do not have today any predilection to impose their views on others. Mutual aid is not derived from the precepts of any religion but rather from a banal observation: I can help you today, you can help me tomorrow. In the severe Finnish climate, survival without the aid of another person was almost impossible. So there is social capital which is based on basic human solidarity, the elemental desire to survive, without any 'enhancements' in the form of religion or ideology. However, the Finnish model seems too idyllic to be able to use among people obsessed with ego and self-interest. Oppression and violence in the city are obvious. They constitute the city. But when speaking of oppression or violence, I do not mean the force that causes suffering but rather the power that liberates. The same strength that turns taps on for water, the same force that chops wood or cuts people's heads open. Power and oppression thus have a moral dimension – they can be good or evil.

City as a Political Idea

If we can mention Hobbes' *Leviathan* in the context of the overarching structure that governs the city, there will be always the question: whose interests does it represent? Who, in a city full of conflicting interests (even if they do not actively conflict), will it support? The fact that urban oppression and violence – which we need if we do not want an uncontrollable city, a city which is an area of chaos and war between these conflicting interests, a city that is *de facto* not a City – always has a colour, always represents an ideology, is the biggest difficulty. On the one hand we know that there is no 'worldview neutrality', but on the other hand some kind of neutrality – or an equal distance from all worldviews and collective interests – is essential if cities are to avoid easily becoming machines of servitude to certain social groups who reign over the others. In traditional political thought there was the construct of the sovereign, the king – a universal force that exists over and above the conflicting parties, representing the interests of the entire community. However, this concept has been challenged and we must recognise that it is not true and does not work. Indeed, if this universal force would be empowered outside the city – within the state or some universal idea, whether religious or ideological – we could for a moment believe in its efficiency. But, besides ideological legitimacy, this authority must have *real* support outside the city and, if so, the city once again ceases to exist as an autonomous power and political idea. The particularity and individualism of the City, as an idea which – as Pierre Manent wrote – has steadily been losing the universality of Church and Empire, means that the City will never become a viable alternative to those existing on the outside, but only to 'agents' existing on the inside.

The residents of the city prefer to trust and be loyal to the forces that previously fought against the City, in order to wrest control of it and make it their slave. Of course, instead of talking about 'empty violence' that should belong to the City as an institution, we could preach the idea that the community can exist outside the institutions. That institutional violence is not necessary and that the community can not only justify its own existence, but also include all the mechanisms of self-control within itself. The problem is that examples of communities existing outside the institutions can be observed in the chaos-stricken regions of Africa. So even though I preach the superiority of self-control and social organisation over control enforced from the outside, I can find no examples showing the possibility of a community that is not subjected to external pressure.

The cases which I describe, where self-organisation has occurred, have always followed in the wake of some external oppression. Therefore, instead of looking for solutions that have already proved their utopianism, I suggest modifying the existing system. I suggest using the mechanisms that already exist and operate. Instead of revolution, I invariably suggest piracy. Instead of destroying – 'hacking' the System. So how do we deprive external oppression of colour, flavour and form without denying its power and effectiveness? There are some concepts, some entities, which may give rise to the outlook necessary for the functioning of 'empty (neutral) violence' in the City. Here, I wish to explore two of these concepts: the 'homeland' and the 'absolute'. The homeland, the national state, is associated with nationalism and ethnic violence, while the notion of the absolute in turn provokes an absolutist ethics of one truth and in consequence (religious) violence. But not necessarily; the homeland and the absolute also exist as the amalgamations of concepts. Yes, 'there are the accounts of injustices in the homeland', but the homeland itself is a vague concept with fuzzy edges, into which everyone puts whatever they want. And yet 'homeland' unites, despite the fact it should not and that no one quite knows what it means, precisely because it is an open, fuzzy concept. It is a similar case with the 'absolute'. If we do not enter any dogmatic religion but still share a belief in the absolute, then we are able to communicate despite the fact that each of us actually yearns for something different.

As Piotr Uklanksi said, "With time I came to the conclusion that the greater challenge is to find an image that would be exhausted in its reception, and to make it something in which people are able to invest their feelings. In this sense, a sunset, 'solidarity' and the Pope have a common denominator. If they were filled with explicit content, it would be difficult to change their meaning depending on context."[76] Such must be the nature of 'empty violence' in the ideological sense – it must be nondescript but powerful. This must also apply to neutral urban spaces and the City Centre itself. This must be the ideological basis of urban violence: undefined but powerful, a bag into which every resident will put their hopes and dreams. As I explained in the previous chapters, local communities living in neighbourhoods or enclaves are a kind of pre-urban relic of clan mentality. Despite the sense of security and 'rooting' offered to their residents, in most cases they become an oppressive and destructive environment for the City as a whole. It is clear that I am not trying to opt for a homogeneous, featureless structure (we see this in tower block estates), but rather – recalling the description of the desired enclave – I am suggesting we create a tension between what is rooted and what is revolutionary. Instead of the oppression of small, local communities, which in their completely degenerate form become closed districts or gang-ruled areas (these are, contrary to appearances, two sides of the same coin), I would opt for a kind of fuzzy city. Here, I would like to repeat the metaphor of fluid dynamics that I introduced earlier. The city is a kind of heterogeneous reservoir, filled with fluids which sometimes mix but mostly do not. These fluids are of different densities and the city therefore exists in flows. Nothing is fixed and forever certain. Imbalance in one place causes flows and fluctuations in another. And now let us drop this metaphor and try another: the City is an Exchange Machine in which the medium is people, who must remain in motion. Rooting is necessary for us but, as I wrote in the beginning, only rooting in the whole of the city – not in a single district. Disintegration into independent, autonomous districts, a clear example of which is Los Angeles, was considered by postmodern urban planners as a desirable solution. In my view – and here the traditionalists will probably agree with me – this kind of disintegration is a disintegration of the City. The New Polis is the inverse of Los Angeles; the New Polis needs an implosion and a powerful centre. There is a belief still lingering among some planners about the existence of what they call 'neutral space'. I remember that, while working on the project for Shankill Road, when we left the district I was told by the director of my company in Belfast that we were now going to the *neutral city space.*

In his book *Recombinant Urbanism,* David Shane uses three elements to describe the city.[77] There is the *armature,* which comprises – in general – all communication routes in the city and is related to movement and flow. Then there is the *enclave*, a static, monofunctional district. Finally, there is a kind of space known as *heterotopia* which does not fit the general pattern of enclaves – it can be, for example, a prison, hospital or factory. Shane assumes, and here I agree with him, that exchange and interaction are 'natural' for the city. There is a relationship between enclaves and communication routes, between what is static and what is dynamic. Through the 'armature', enclaves communicate with each other. So if the enclaves may possess content – in the model presented by Shane – then routes are only neutral spaces through which content leaks into the enclaves. However, in reality the neutrality of routes is so theoretical that it is actually false. The famous Parisian boulevards, designed by Baron Haussmann, are a perfect example. Boulevards represent an obvious ideology – the ideology of aristocratic power. A beautiful, functional, aristocratic city was imposed on the dirty, working class and plebeian lanes of the 'old' Paris. Contrary to what is taught to architecture students, Haussmann's Paris did not abolish the 'bad', dirty Paris. Boulevards cut the old tissue but in themselves became firewalls, through which people living within the blocks had their possibility of movement hindered. And so it is always and everywhere – a 'neutral' space is in fact the space of dominant ideology. What is beyond the 'boulevards' is private, divided, individual and weak. It does not matter, the message is obvious – the streets are important. Space which is called 'public', or even just 'neutral', is the space which is fought over.

Whoever appropriates this space appropriates the entire city. Here we can go back to the famous ban of the Equality March in Poznań, 2006. The dominant ideology in Poland (and certainly in Poznań) is a conservative consumerism. 'Neutral space', however, is not necessarily oppressive in principle – on the contrary, 'neutral space' is the space of a compromise. This space can be a space of liberal-democratic utopia, it can be a space of petty-bourgeois consensus. However, this neutrality is guaranteed only to the extent acceptable by the dominant ideology in the City. That is why, as I repeat again, the political dimension of the city is at the core of any urban crises and all disputes relating to this space. This space, which we used to regard as neutral and which is obviously not, could become something more – something much more important and more honest. Yet the existence of 'neutral space' in Belfast has nothing to do with the problems that lurk in Shankill. The strategy that the city applies to the 'troublesome' areas is the creation of enclaves – heterotopia. It cuts these parts off and forgets about them. Kowloon Walled City was a fragment of Hong Kong formally established on land belonging to China. Therefore, the local Hong Kong law did not apply and it became a place inhabited by squatters and other marginalised communities (including immigrants and criminals, of course). What was unusual in KWC, which was destroyed just before the annexation of Hong Kong by China, was its incredible density of development (and thus population) – 13,000 people per hectare. The density was about 150 times higher than in New York. It is difficult, however, to compare the two – after all, KWC was actually a building. KWC was probably the only structure of this type (i.e. formed without any plan, design or control) which was layered. KWC was a multi-storey megastructure. It is interesting to note that playgrounds for children were located on the roof of this structure – is it not a fantastic proof of the prevalence of avant-garde solutions? Although, if anyone is a fan of cyberpunk then in KWC they will definitely find the cyberpunk archetype of many landscapes, including scenery from the film *Johnny Mnemonic*. Once again, this structure was created without architects or plans and was ruled by the community itself. KWC had no formal authority (though the real 'power structure' was, of course, present). Hoi Chiu, who grew up in KWC, recalled: "It is amazing that it all worked. It was because people were forced to work together. This meant that KWC could function." The social mechanism described by Hoi Chiu is similar to the one that governed the functioning of the community in People's Poland blocks. Tower block estates also functioned because people were forced to cooperate, but there the external forces of oppression inquired inside the community. In KWC, the 'dangerous' and 'oppressive' remained on the outside. Inside, there was only free cooperation.

This anarchic urban tissue was not unique and could be seen in other countries. In 1963, Jan Minorski wrote that, even in Poland, we had to deal with the phenomenon of 'spontaneous architecture' after the war."[78] Buildings in post-war Poland were 'growing' through the extension of new accommodations over the pre-existing ones. KWC had done the same, only vertically. In Poland, though, we had no chance of an anarchist social structure with which to populate such 'spontaneous architecture'. Despite their fascinating spatial form, such human habitats seem all the more interesting as models of autonomous communities. Communities that have undergone external coercion, while maintaining their inner freedom (as far as possible), can function quite successfully. Here, of course, the question of 'social capital' returns once again. All of these communities, despite the fact that they look anarchist, are internally heavily oppressive. Social capital has – as I have written many times – its light and dark sides.

That anarchist authoritarian model, however, remains fascinating to me. Can such a model be used in the modern, democratic cities of the West? There were, after all, neighbourhoods like Christiania in Copenhagen, where within a structured (but very liberal) social system a socio-spatial experiment was undertaken. Moreover, such districts were eventually 'taken over' (at least in some sense) by the neoliberal system. Could such 'anarchist' neighbourhoods become a part of 'civilised' cities? As autonomous entities in their own right? Does the system allow the existence of such holes, or safety valves, in itself? Probably not – unless the system creates and programs those 'holes' itself, peeling from them any anti-systemic dimension. And this is the direction in which Florida's theory of the creative class moves. Capitalism devours everything. Social capital disappears, leaving only the capital. And apparently the majority likes it.

To sum up: there are two types of oppression in the city. The first is genetically pre-urban oppression – a sectarian, conformist oppression that binds people, tethers their hearts, minds and consciences. The second type of oppression comes from the city itself, representing all that the city is and how it differs from other communities. This second type of oppression is one that forces us to meet, interact and collaborate. Strangely and paradoxically, the first type of oppression comes from within the community while the second comes mostly from the exterior. On the surface this observation invalidates everything I have written so far, because if the essence of urbanity is supposed to be the autonomy of the urban community – which originates from the interior of this community – then the logical conclusion would be to promote sectarian, xenophobic enclaves as communities truly deriving their strength from within themselves and thus truly urban. The second kind of oppression – as a force 'attacking' residents of the City from the 'outside' – would then have more in common with imperial oppression, which is precisely what I am trying to resist in this book. Most of today's urban planners and politicians are under this illusion. It is this erroneous thinking that strengthens the processes which are disintegrating the City and privatising its space. Even the neoliberal city, which in theory does not take into account the existence of local communities, operates based on the market needs of its residents who are quite often – particularly in big cities, or 'Molochs' – grouped in closed enclaves which are ethnically, nationally and economically defined. I do not like organic metaphors, but this sounds like a liberation movement for legs or kidneys. Neither legs nor kidneys can exist by themselves. Similarly, neither can the urban districts.

The aforementioned regeneration plan of the Shankill Road district in Belfast takes into account all the wishes of the people living there, ignoring the fact that in the shadows next door lurk developers who have a very different plan for this district. The Shankill Road regeneration project ignored the fact that this district is a part of the city – a part of a larger whole. Therefore, when talking about oppression in the city, the community's self-awareness and the self-governance of its residents, let us not make the mistake of scale. Oppression and violence in a separate portion of the city – a local oppression – is like a cramp in the leg. Urban oppression, the kind of oppression that I see as the foundation of the City, is like the contraction of the muscles which make us move, step and turn our heads – the muscle that pumps blood around our bodies. We can learn much from the oppression of small communities. This kind of oppression forces a direct relationship between one human being and another. Urban oppression is a system of oppression that forces people to consider such relationships.

Krzysztof Nawratek

IV.V   THE REBUILDING OF POLIS

The fundamental question is – how are we to root the consumer in the city? How are we to make a Plug-in Citizen out of the consumer? How are we to give people a sense of being 'at home' without giving them a xenophobic identity? How are we to 'hook' people who do not live in the city permanently but who are, were or want to be associated with it? I gave a lecture at the National Gallery in Warsaw, early in 2007, entitled *In Search of a Post-neoliberal City: Belfast – Shanghai – Riga*. In this lecture I said, among other things, that the ultimate goal of my work, my writing and thinking is to rebuild the City as a functioning and effective political idea. By 'political idea', of course, I mean the model reminiscent of Greek Polis – a community living in a defined territory which is self-conscious enough to be able to manage itself. But today, would this new Polis just be a kind of autonomous city – maybe a city-state such as Singapore? I do not believe so. One of the most important disputes in today's world concerns the proponents of globalisation as the dominant idea (whether good or bad) and those who believe that the national state still has meaning and power (again, without evaluating whether it is good or bad). This argument reminds me of a dispute which lies at the root of modern Europe: the dispute between the universalist idea of the Church and the more particular idea of the Kingdom. The question that is crucial for me is whether there might be space for the idea of the City between these two – whether there is room for the a-a City, the City of Plug-in Citizens. It appears that there is not, but this is not quite true. As Pierre Manent wrote, the city is too narrow, too individual to be an alternative to the Empire or the national state. Yet, the struggle for the City as a *viable* alternative to both the oppressive national state and the Empire – bureaucratic beyond human imagination – is, in my opinion, a risk worth taking. I believe that an unexpected opportunity for the City has arrived because the City, as I see and interpret it – that is, as a City of Plug-in Citizens – is no more particular than the national state but neither is it weaker. It is different – somewhat stronger and more efficient than either State or Empire. It both determines and beats its two competitors in the field.

The a-a City, which is the new Polis, exists in at least two dimensions. There is the specific geographical area and location of the City, and then there is the non-geographic aspect of the City – specific *characteristics* of the City, a certain founding myth based on a particular ideology (and the exclusion of others). The City is therefore more concrete, more 'tangible' and more 'ours' than the national state (geographically) and gives us the chance to build a local community, while at the same time (non-geographically) there are quite specific characteristics which determine the individual and unique life of the City itself. Again, the City is a community existing not only in space, in a particular place, but 'everywhere'. It is the City that becomes the network of a particular community in the world, the material realisation of abstract ideas. The a-a City's advantage over both the State and the Empire lies in the ease of its potential existence as a Community. The advantage of the City lies – paradoxically – in its particularity. The City does not claim universalism, refuses to yield to the ambition of embracing the rest of the world, but remains universal in its assumptions, axioms and values.

The City exists, therefore, both as a place and as an idea. The a-a City exists as a definite and defined *slice* of reality – both in physical and abstract space. However, in contrast to sectarian villages, monasteries or ethnic enclaves, the City is an open, self-governing and self-sufficient organism. Open; because, as I wrote when characterising the concept of the Plug-in Citizen, any person can become a part of it. Self-governing; because the power which comes from within the community is the foundation of the City itself. Self-sufficient; because self-sufficiency is the only viable political path for the City – but self-sufficiency does not mean autarky. Self-sufficiency means the freedom of choice in selecting partners. It also means that through the Plug-in Citizens, Cities become entities with their agents anywhere on the planet and these 'agents' enable the self-sufficiency of the city. The a-a City is a kind of Deleuzian machine – it works in a particular place, for a particular purpose and based on a specified diagram. The paradoxical power of the a-a City comes from the strength of the Plug-in Citizens. The fact that they are only 'sometimes' residents of the physical city is irrelevant. They are involved in the bloodstream of the City in such a way that they are fully adhered to it without necessarily being the City's (physical) residents. They are thus 'agents' of the City, providing it with information, funds and knowledge, representing it in other Cities and other places. Despite its limitations (in terms of location and its specified way of 'experiencing' the world) the formula of the a-a City is extremely roomy. The concept of a-androgyny, based on lack and imperfection, has endless possibilities for development. The a-a City, the new Polis, becomes a community which is more 'spiritual' than territorial. Its territoriality is potential – it gives its Plug-in Citizens an anchor, the ability to root in the world, but it is a flexible and completely voluntary kind of rooting.

Of course, it is only the potential of the community and we have to be very careful to never forget the definition of the urban community formulated by Aristotle – that the City is built with various people and that people who are alike cannot build a city. But this is precisely the idea of the a-a City and a-androgynous space. Thus, despite the fact that the City tends towards a certain integrity – a narrowing of the range of ways in which one can experience and re-live life – the idea of a-androgyny combats this potential homogeneity. These two contradictory trends – one aiming to unify the city and the other striving for constant and radical incompleteness – guarantee the viability and flexibility of the a-a City. If money is a medium by which people in the neoliberal city communicate, then a fundamental task in the construction of the a-a City is to broaden the field of communication.

There cannot be a worse opinion of the tradition of 'subbotniks' than there is today in Poland. In fact, it is hard to imagine anyone in Eastern Europe taking the idea of subbotniks seriously. Despite this, I think it is worth looking at what we unthinkingly reject. The consumer's relationship with the neoliberal city is based on money but none of us want to be reduced to mere consumers. We do not want to be simply a mouth, digestive tract and credit card. If so, what can we offer besides money? If we don't want to be thus reduced, we must extend the field of communication as much as we can. Instead of money, we need to tie up the City with our Life. Biopolitics raises chills of fear and can be seen as the root of all totalitarianism.[79] Maybe we should redefine biopolitics? To Aristotle, a human being was a cluster of biological essence and political essence – and biopolitics caused the fusion of these two entities. But why do we think that Aristotle was right? Why is division truer than integrity? The reduction of a person to their wallet is a simple consequence of the division of the human being into the biological and the political. But a human being is an integral whole – a collection of processes, properties and characteristics. Yes, we can separate the different parts of a human being – but what for? If we admit that the political being, as something with a specific and 'separate' kind of existence in the world, is something bizarre and that it was this division of the human being into pieces which led to a degradation of what is not political – that is, the biological body (the aforementioned case of a Nigerian woman raped and tortured in Poland is an all too painful example of this) – then we can get back to thinking about the Plug-in Citizens and their *plugging in* to the city without prior prejudice.

To reiterate – the city of late capitalism plugs people into itself through money. A person is a consumer and nothing more. What may expand the *plugging field* (because I'm not saying that we should abandon money – that would be absurd!) is everything else that is part of human being. Part of life. Such as, for example, time. Here we return to the ineffective 'subbotniks' on the one hand, and on the other to one of the anti-capitalist technologies: so-called 'time banks'. Is time one of the mediums by which we plug into the city? These two examples show that this is true. However, since the a-a City is based on lacks, of which there are infinitely many, then the variety of mediums we can use is infinite. Time, however, is a clear, concrete example of broad connotations. I do not want to vulgarise this issue, but we can treat time as a means of payment in which the city collects the tax. All that the City and its inhabitants are missing may be remitted by the other Plug-in Citizens to the City as a 'tax'. If you define the a-a City as a way of experiencing the world that is common to all its Citizens, then it becomes obvious that experiencing – that life itself – is what brings people together with the City. Older citizens, pensioners, can often have a surplus of time. Their way of plugging in to the City could be to give their time – in terms of their memories and life experiences, as well as physically being with others – to those who are often short of it.

Therefore, the a-a City, this new Polis, is a biopolitical machine. The City manages its capital, which is largely human capital, in the most literal sense. Human capital management is both the management of the time of City residents and the management of their bodies. All philosophical discussions about abortion, genetic engineering – and probably human hybridisation or cyborgs soon enough – should be resolved within the City. So if one of the main objectives that I have set myself, in order to proclaim a vision of the a-a City, is to promote diversity, then this diversity cannot simply be restricted to the colour and brand of one's socks but must embrace the biological basis of existence. Since, however, the a-a City is an 'empty oppression', it really is not so much the case that the City manages its human resources, but rather that it is forcing each of its Plug-in Citizens to manage their own Life. This constraint, this 'empty oppression', is one of the fundamental characteristics of the a-a City.

A-ANDROGYNIC SPACE   IV.VI
In Search of a Post-neoliberal City Model

It is time to properly introduce the a-androgynous City and a model of its space. This scheme is based on two basic ideas: the idea of lack as value and the idea of flow as connection. The former is the basic ideological assumption here and the latter is the primary technique used in this model. So what is meant by my statement that the City is based on shortcomings? Each enclave (a part of a town with its own particularity) is, by definition, incomplete. The complements to their deficiencies can be found in the adjacent enclaves and in the a-androgynous corridors – that is, 'public' spaces – managed by the City, and which form the basic machinery which forces interactions.

A-a corridors combine boulevards, communication networks and so-called 'centre-enabling functions'. Spatially, a-a corridors are a kind of 'negative' street; they are structures rather than open spaces but movement still takes place within them – both longitudinal and transversal. However, this movement is due not so much to the enclaves which are adjacent to the a-a corridors as to the corridors themselves. They have the power to attract and draw people from their enclaves. On the surface, enclaves are self-sufficient – like Chinese or Jewish quarters, or Catholic and Protestant districts in Belfast. In reality, however, this self-sufficiency is crippled. For it is based on partial fullness and only partial excellence. A tentative, if trivial, solution to this was proposed (but ultimately not adopted) in the conflict zone between two communities in the Shankill Road district. Between them was a classic square – a 'neutral' public space – and one side of this square was to be invested with children's playgrounds while the other with small shops. In this case the imperfection, or 'lack', would have been an element which dynamised the structure – dynamised it to change. A trivial solution, but one forcing the conflicting communities to interact – not in a 'neutral' space but in a space seemingly defined as either 'ours' or 'theirs'. Seemingly, because this space is still encroached upon by the City – as a machine which manages interactions – despite being under the private ownership of the conflicting communities. Of course, somewhere in the background the conflict still exists but under these circumstances it does not constitute a problem. Nor is it the case that the a-a City reinforces conflicts – rather, it seeks to sublimate them, tear them from ideology, leaving only 'empty oppression'. What is an a-androgynous corridor? It is the basic building material of the a-a City, it is one of the possible materialisations of the city's 'empty violence' and it is a medium for the enforcement of communication between enclaves.

To further understand the idea of the a-a corridor we must go back to Hausmann's famous reconstruction of Paris. David Harvey writes: "The new boulevards were designed as public spaces to help the state to protect the private property of the bourgeoisie. Therefore, they were not be available for those who would undermine the bourgeois social order, or at least seem to challenge it, by showing their rags."[80] So, contrary to what is considered customary on the Parisian boulevards, their 'publicness' was specific. In a sense, Hausmann created the bourgeois Paris, overwriting the existing city, and therein lies the (evil) genius of his scheme – the poor and the marginalised did not disappear from Paris but, through the construction of boulevards, the natural paths through which these people moved and communicated with each other were torn apart and shredded. The poor became trapped within the spaces between the boulevards. So the boulevards became corridors through which the life of the city ran, but this life simply slipped past the facades of the city without even trying to penetrate the interior. A-a corridors are to some extent the inverse of Haussmann's boulevards. For if, in the case of Haussmann's boulevards, we were dealing primarily with movement along the facades, then the a-a corridors exist primarily as the space between the built environments – between the enclaves. Despite the fact that they move goods, people and information along their sides, their core function is to 'force' enclaves to communicate. The weakening and linearity of cities, the introduction of one-way systems, results primarily from the vehicular transport system, which is why the only valid model for the a-a City is, above all, public and pedestrian transport. Private cars are therefore completely eliminated from the interior of the a-a city, and only the emergency services (fire brigade, police, ambulance) and taxis (necessary for people with disabilities, the elderly, etc.) can move around the city without special restrictions. Public transport systems also have freedom of movement but these have a different impact on the urban space of the city – pedestrians confront this system at stops and stations, drivers confront it on the roads and at crossings. The ideal type of public transport is the metro but any other kind of mass public transport system, such as the 'supertram' in northern England, plays a similar role and functions in a similar way.

A-a corridors are, above all, the materialisation of 'empty oppression' – this means that they contain the supra-district functions (schools, nurseries, offices, larger shops, sports grounds, etc.) as well as open up areas in a restricted manner. Open spaces are too weak in themselves because they seldom play the powerful, 'oppressive' role required to force interaction, and that is why they should be located within the enclaves – where the integrated community can give them a proper meaning. So enclaves 'plug' into the a-a corridors in order to take from them the 'life fluids' necessary for their existence. A-a corridors operate between enclaves but also interfere with the 'inside' of the enclaves themselves. No enclave can exist 'outside' the system of a-a corridors – they penetrate the enclaves. The 'privacy' of the enclaves is still challenged by the 'publicness' of the corridors. The first, yet very shy, use of a-a corridors was proposed by a group called 'Riga Deserves Better' in their alternative model for the spatial development of Riga – 'Ring', as in a kind of 'peripheral centre'. This Ring included both communication corridors (both rail and motor transport) and the centre-enabling functions. The task of the Ring was to pull all activity which had spread beyond the Ring back towards the historic centre of the city and thus block any further urban sprawl in Riga.

The third element of the a-a City – after enclaves and a-a corridors – is 'plug-in sockets', or areas through which the City can 'plug in' to the world and the surrounding region (which in turn can 'plug in' to the City). These sockets are, of course, airports, seaports, railways and coach stations. In the centre of the a-a City is... the Centre. Yes, the a-a City does have a Center, which is an accumulation of corridors and, above all, is functionally linked to the main plug-in sockets. The centre is the place at which tourists and migrant workers arrive, who do not often venture beyond it. But of course the Centre also serves the residents, who can come into contact with the world – come into contact with 'strangers'. If the role of a-a corridors is to provoke interaction between the enclaves, then the primary role of the Centre is to 'force' the City's interaction with the 'outside'.

At the ends of a-a corridors, on the outskirts of the City, there are plug-in sockets of regional significance. There are also nodes for the park-and-ride system, parking for personal transport, local railways and similar functions. Two key questions remain: first, about the scale of the City. When we construct a model, it mostly has specific boundary conditions. So the question is whether the model of the a-a City is as good for a small town, where thirty thousand people live, as it is for a city of three million inhabitants? The second question concerns the region. What is the relationship between the a-a City and the surrounding region? Why should we go back to the concept of the City today, when no one seriously considers the city as separate from the region in which it is located? To answer the first doubt: I think that this model is more of an algorithm than a model in the classical sense. As I said, it must be interpreted as a Deleuzian diagram. Therefore, a more detailed description would concern the rules and general regulations but, as it happens with diagrams, each materialisation of the model is different, every City is unique. If we consider as fundamental the issue of self-sufficiency and self-governance in the City, then size is of secondary importance.

Why a city and not a region? Because a region has no boundaries. A region is an area which we can describe better in terms of the intensity of interaction rather than with the appointment of clear boundaries. A city needs a border to be able to define itself. In some sense, however, the a-a City does not have a limit – if we speak about the characteristics of the city, of the City as an idea. But when we speak about a specific, physically and geographically situated city – then limits are necessary. Yes, the a-a City may be present throughout the world through its Plug-in Citizens, but the physical city is a specific, delineated space – it is *here* and not *there*. The division between Polis and the 'outsiders' is an archaic division, but it must not be entirely rejected if we do not want to lose the fundamental value of the new Polis – the ability to root its citizens.

Technical questions still remain – about the media, the warehouses, the factories, the landfill sites. The answer is radical: everything has to fit and balance within the city limits. The a-a City is not merely a social phenomenon – the lack and incompleteness of its ideological foundation relates to each element of the City's functioning. The a-a City is not only a political project – it is also a response to the threat of climate change, the challenge of oil shortage and other such problems – but the political dimension of the a-a City is crucial in making it at all possible to deal with these fundamental problems.

Happy People in Their Own City   IV.VII

The a-a City is a hub. That was always the essence of Polis, the essence of the City throughout the ages. Today (and tomorrow?) the new Polis is a chance to be rooted in real and concrete space without having to reside in this space, while at the same time giving this possibility to its citizens. Polis exists at both the virtual level, as a concept of political identity, and the physical level, as a specific city in a particular space. The interpenetration of these two spaces – physical and virtual – creates the unique character of the a-a City. This feature allows us to be co-participants in the City (Plug-in Citizens) no matter where we reside, no matter what language we use or what our ethnicity is. We can even decide to never actually live in the physical city and still be deeply rooted Plug-in Citizens. This is possible because being a co-participant of the a-a City is primarily *being rooted* in a particular *community*. Since participation in the community is based on the concept of the a-androgyne – that is, an imperfect, incomplete human being, a human of 'lack' – and the manner in which participation in the urban community is negotiated depends both on the individual and their particular a-a City, there are hardly any conditions that prevent anyone from being a Plug-in Citizen in any city. We must also remember that every relationship – every act of 'plugging in' to an a-a City – is different.

Cities, however, differ between themselves by the algorithms that manage their internal structures. The number of possible permutations resulting from the combination of these algorithms is infinite – as infinite as the human imagination. Finally, the intermingling of communities existing in both the symbolic and physical dimensions gives the a-a City – the new Polis – a universal dimension, without depriving it of its communal particularism.

The New Polis becomes, therefore, a universal model, but not one which defines the unique character of each case. Each City is then a Machine with specific algorithms that govern its inner workings while maintaining the 'universal language of the surface', which is in fact the interface allowing different people and different districts to communicate. This 'universal language of the surface' is a negotiable medium of exchange and communication both within and between individual Cities. The algorithms of each City also govern – above all, perhaps – the concept of the Plug-In Citizen, which can (theoretically) be plugged in to more than one Machine, more than one Polis. And what is the purpose of all this? It is to enable people in the City to fully re-live their lives. Maybe even to allow them to be happy.

City as a Political Idea

v.

After

Krzysztof Nawratek

The book you are holding in your hands, dear Reader, is not primarily a critical book. It is not a polemic, nor even a description of the world. This book is a projection, or at least a sketch, of the a-androgynous City.

I do not like the world in which we live. I believe that we can afford to improve it. But I do not want a revolution – I am not looking for solutions in the drastic changes, upheavals, wars and violence that cause human suffering. On the contrary, the project that I propose, though radical in concept and purpose, is delicate in its strategy and method. As I have written, I do not propose an open war with the System – I suggest instead a subtle 'hacking'. But alone – even as a potential Plug-in Citizen, plugged in to the systems of several Cities – I am nothing. Every project is teamwork. The bigger the project, the more hands and minds there are needed to put it into practice. I am hoping for your help.

Endnotes

II. INVISIBLE

II.I · CITIZENSHIP

1. See Y. Soysal, *Limits of Citizenship: Migrants and Postnational Membership in Europe* (Chicago: University of Chicago Press, 1994); or *Immigration and the Politics of Citizenship in Europe and North America*, ed. by R. Brubaker (Lanham: University Press of America, 1989).

2. N. Rose and C. Novas, 'Biological Citizenship', in *GlobalAssemblages: Technology, Politics, and Ethics as Anthropological Problems*, ed. by A. Ong and S. Collier (Oxford: Blackwell Publishing, 2005), pp. 439-463.

3. V. FitzGerald and J. Cuesta-Leiva, 'The Economic Value of a Passport: A Model of Citizenship and the Social Dividend in a Global Economy', *QEH Working Papers* <http://ideas.repec.org/p/qeh/qehwps/qehwps04.html>.

4. T. Marshall and T. Bottomore, *Citizenship and Social Class* (London: Pluto Press, 1987).

5. M. Purcell, 'Citizenship and the Right to the Global City: Reimagining the Capitalist World Order', *International Journal of Urban and Regional Research*, 27 (2003), 564-590.

6. J. Jenson and M. Papillon, 'The Changing Boundaries of Citizenship: A Review and a Research Agenda', in *Modernising Governance: A Preliminary Exploration* (Ottawa: Canadian Centre for Management Development, 2000).

7. J. Lepofsky and J. Fraser, 'Building Community Citizens: Claiming the Right to Place-making in the City', *Urban Studies*, 40 (2003), 127-142.

8. C. Joppke, 'How Immigration Is Changing Citizenship: A Comparative View', *Ethnic and Racial Studies*, 22 (1999), 629-652.

9. C. Needham, *Citizen-Consumers: New Labour's Marketplace Democracy* (London: The Catalyst Forum, 2003).

II.II · CITY AS A POLITICAL COMMUNITY. DEATH OF POLIS

10. P. Manent, *An Intellectual History of Liberalism*, trans. by R. Balinski (Princeton: Princeton University Press, 1994).

11. H. Lefebvre, 'The Right to the City', in *Writings on Cities*, trans. by E. Kofman and E. Lebas (Oxford: Blackwell, 1996).

12. M. Purcell, 'Excavating Lefebvre: The Right to the City and its Urban Politics of the Inhabitant', *GeoJournal*, 58 (2002), 99-108.

13. G. Agamben, *Homo Sacer: Sovereign Power and Bare Life*, trans. by D. Heller-Roazen (Stanford: Stanford University Press, 1998).

14. M. Edwards, 'Global Civil Society and Community Exchanges: A Different Form of Movement', *Environment and Urbanisation*, 13 (2001), 145-149.

15. S. Žižek, *The Puppet and the Dwarf: The Perverse Core of Christianity* (Cambridge: MIT Press, 2003).

16. J. Staniszkis, *O Władzy i Bezsilności* (Kraków: Wydawnictwo Literackie, 2006).

II.III · STRANGERS IN THE CITY. IMMIGRANTS AS ATTRACTION, IMMIGRANTS AS MENACE

17 L. Hoffman, 'The Marketing of Diversity in the Inner City: Tourism and Regulation in Harlem', *International Journal of Urban and Regional Research*, 27 (2003), 286-299.

18 E. Bonacich, 'A Theory of Middleman Minorities', *American Sociological Review*, 38 (1973), 583-594.

19 D. Judd, 'Visitors and the Spatial Ecology of the City', in *Cities and Visitors: Regulating People, Markets, and City Space*, ed. by L. Hoffman, S. Fainstein and D. Judd (Malden: Blackwell Publishing, 2003), pp. 23-38.

II.IV · SOCIAL CAPITAL

20 E. Glaeser, 'The Future of Urban Research: Non-market Interactions', *Brookings-Wharton Papers on Urban Affairs*, 1 (2000), 101-138.

21 A. Ong, *Neoliberalism as Exception: Mutations in Citizenship and Sovereignty* (Durham: Duke University Press, 2006).

22 R. Florida, *Cities and the Creative Class* (London: Routledge, 2005).

23 M. Levitt, *Hamas: Politics, Charity, and Terrorism in the Service of Jihad* (New Haven: Yale University Press, 2006).

24 M. Dikec, *Badlands of the Republic: Space, Politics and Urban Policy* (Malden: Wiley-Blackwell, 2007).

25 P. Elmlund, 'The Vital Businesses of Immigrants', *Axess*, 4 (2005).

II.V · FALL OF THE PERIPHERAL CITIES. DISPOSABLE CITIES

26 There is a whole research project concerning the phenomenon of shrinking cities online: <http://www.shrinkingcities.com>.

II.VI · CITY MANAGEMENT. MANAGERIAL GOVERNANCE AGAINST 'THE LOCAL COMMUNITY'

27 M. Hansen, Polis: *An Introduction to the Ancient Greek City-State* (Oxford: Oxford University Press, 2006).

28 P. Tai, 'Social Polarisation: Comparing Singapore, Hong Kong and Taipei', *Urban Studies*, 43 (2006), 1737-1756.

29 G. Baiocchi, 'Participation, Activism, and Politics: The Porto Alegre Experiment and Deliberative Democratic Theory', *Politics and Society*, 29 (2001), 43-72.

30 R. Górski, *Bez Państwa: Demokracja Uczestnicząca w Działaniu* (Kraków: Korporacja Ha!art, 2007).

31 D. Harvey, *A Brief History of Neoliberalism* (Oxford: Oxford University Press, 2005).

II.VII · 'DISPERSED' POWER AGAINST 'REAL' POWER

32 Vladimir Mayakovsky, 'Vladimir Ilyich Lenin' (1924).

33   J. Fairbank and M. Goldman, *China: A New History*, 2nd edn (Cambridge: Belknap Press, 1998).

34   J. Staniszkis, *Władza Globalizacji* (Warsaw: Wydawnictwo Naukowe Scholar, 2003).

35   E. Levinas, *Time and the Other and Additional Essays*, trans. by R. Cohen (Pittsburgh: Duquesne University Press, 1987).

36   A. Bielik-Robson, How To Philosophize with a Hammer, "Dziennik" daily, "Euroep" supplement, issue 6/7/2007.

II.VIII · PLUG-IN CITIZEN AS A PREREQUISITE FOR THE RESURRECTION OF POLIS. POLIS AS A DEFENSE AND LIBERATION

37   G. Mirandola, 'Oration on the Dignity of Man' (1486) <http://www.mnstate.edu/gracyk/courses/web%20publishing/pico_oration.htm>.

38   Vladimir Mayakovsky, 'Vladimir Ilyich Lenin' (1924).

39   B. Frey, 'Flexible Citizenship for a Global Society', *Politics, Philosophy and Economics*, 2 (2003), 93-114.

40   N. Smith, *The New Urban Frontier: Gentrification and the Revanchist City* (London: Routledge, 1996).

41   K. Ward, 'Entrepreneurial Urbanism: State Restructuring and Civilising "New" East Manchester', *Area*, 35 (2003), 116-127.

III. INTIMATE

III.I · THE INHABITANT OF A PERIPHERAL CITY

42   For the Globalisation and World Cities Research Network, see: <http://www.lboro.ac.uk/gawc/index.html>.

43   R. Kallus, 'The Political Role of the Everyday', *City*, 8 (2004), 341-361.

44   'CSO Shows Population Change in Dublin', *RTE News*, 14 June 2007 <http://www.rte.ie/news/2007/0614/migrants.html>.

III.II · EVERYDAY LIFE IN A SUBJECTIVE CITY

45   This chapter has already appeared in a different form within *Miejskie Powitanie* (Warszawa: Biblioteka Wizerunku Miasta, 2007).

46   K. Nawratek, 'Miejscy, nie Miejscowi', *Czas Kultury*, 2 (2005), 30-35.

47   R. Golledge and R. Stimson, *Spatial Behavior: A Geographic Perspective* (New York: Guilford Press, 1997).

III.III · A FUGITIVE FROM A PERIPHERAL CITY

48   S. Sassen, *Guests and Aliens* (New York: New Press, 1999).

III.IV · FREEDOM AND ALIENATION

49   P. Pullman, *Northern Lights; The Subtle Knife; The Amber Spyglass* (London: Scholastic, 1995; 1997; 2000).

III.V · TO LIVE OR SURVIVE

None.

III.VI · THE WORLD IS OURS

50   Z. Bauman, *Wasted Lives: Modernity and its Outcasts* (Cambridge: Polity, 2004).

III.VII · TO EACH THEIR OWN PARADISE

51   N. Stephenson, *The Diamond Age: Or, a Young Lady's Illustrated Primer* (New York: Bantam Books, 1995).

52   F. Herbert, *Dune* (Philadelphia: Chilton Books, 1965).

III.VIII · A PLUG-IN HUMAN BEING, A-ANDROGYNE. PEOPLE HOOKED BY THEIR SHORTCOMINGS

53   Riga City Council, *Riga Development Plan 2006 – 2018* (Riga: City Development Department, 2006).

54   N. Andrews, 'Utopian Androgyny: Romantic Socialist Confront Individualism in July Monarchy France', *French Historical Studies*, 26 (2003), 437-457.

55   E. Głażewska, 'Androgynia – Model Człowieka XXI Wieku', *Annales UMCS*, 16 (2001), 17-28.

56   J. Jacobs, *The Death and Life of Great American Cities* (New York: Random House, 1961).

57   S. Sassen, *The Global City: London, New York, Tokyo* (Princeton: Princeton University Press, 1991).

58   E. Rewers, Post-polis: *Wstęp do Filozofii Ponowoczesnego Miasta* (Kraków: Universitas, 2005).

59   K. Nawratek, *Ideologie w Przestrzeni: Próby Demistyfikacji*, (Kraków: Universitas, 2005).

60   K. Nawratek, 'Wspólnoty Pogardy', *Magazyn Obywatel*, 6 (2005).

61   P. Baxandall and C. Euchner, 'Can CitiStat Work in Greater Boston?', *Harvard University Working Paper No. 7* (2003).

IV. VISIBLE

IV.I · THE SPATIAL STRUCTURE OF SEMI-PERIPHERAL CITIES. A SOCIO-SPATIAL DISINTEGRATION OF A POSTMODERN CITY

62   G. Deleuze, F. Guattari, *Anti-Oedipus. Capitalism and Schizophrenia*, transl. R. Hurley, M. Seem, H.R. Lane, London–New York.

63   S. Sassen, Territory, Authority, Rights: From Medieval to Global Assemblages, Princeton 2006.

64 R. McClintock, 'Cities, Youth and Technology: Toward Pedagogy of Autonomy', *Institute for Learning Technologies* <http://www.ilt.columbia.edu/publications/cities/cyt.html>.

65 D. Läpple, 'Stadt und Region in Zeiten der Globalisierung und Digitalisierung', *Deutsche Zeitschrift fur Kommunalwissenschaften*, 40 (2001).

66 W. Heitmeyer, 'Versagt die "Integrationsmaschine" Stadt?', in *Die Krise der Städte*, ed. by W. Heitmeyer, R. Dollase and O. Backes (Frankfurt: Suhrkamp, 1998).

67 M. Pawley, 'Towards a Digital Disurbanism', *Heise Online* <http://www.heise.de/tp/artikel/6/6031/4.html >.

68 W. Mitchell, *City of Bits: Space, Place and the Infobahn* (Cambridge: MIT Press, 1998).

69 A. Mikhelev, 'City and Poetry: The Interaction between Material and Verbal Signs', *Koht ja Paik/Place and Location 3* (2003), 345-359.

70 A. Zvirgzdins, Editorial, *Latvijas Architektura*, 1 (2005).

IV.II · NEIGHBOURHOOD COMMUNITY IN A SEMI-PERIPHERAL CITY

71 M. Eliade, *The Sacred and the Profane: The Nature of Religion* (Philadelphia: Harvest Books, 1968).

IV.III · THE LOST MYTH OF THE SOCIALIST CITY?

72 A. Bertaud and B. Renaud, 'Cities without Land Markets: Location and Land Use in the Socialist City', *World Bank Policy Research Working Paper No. 1477* (1995).

73 E. Bhatt, 'Questions Mold Our Lives', *CETR* <http://www.cetr.net/en/articles/interviews_and_portraits/questions_mold_our_lives >.

74 E. Bhatt, 'Cities Are People', in WIEGO <http://www.wiego.org/news/events/UPC/Bhatt%20Cities%20are%20People.pdf>.

IV.IV · CITY AS OPPRESSION

75 A. Kearns, 'Social Capital, Regeneration and Urban Policy', *CNR Paper No. 15* (2004).

76 P. Uklanski, 'Solidarity is an Empty Sign', *Gazeta Wyborcza*, 16 June 2007.

77 D. Shane, *Recombinant Urbanism* (Chichester: Wiley-Academy, 2005).

78 J. Minorski, 'Spontaneous Architecture', *Architektura* (1963).

IV.V · THE REBUILDING OF POLIS

79 In 2006, A. Heller gave a series of lectures and seminars in Lublin entitled, 'Biopolitics against Freedom: A New Chapter of the Old Debate'.

IV.VI · A-ANDROGYNIC SPACE. IN SEARCH OF A POST-NEOLIBERAL CITY MODEL

80 D. Harvey, 'The Political Economy of Public Space', in *The Politics of Public Space,* ed. by S. Low and N. Smith (London: Routledge, 2006), pp. 17-34.